COMPUTERISED BOOK

Institute of Certified Bookkeepers

Level II

British Library Cataloguing-in-Publication Data

A catalogue record for this book is available from the British Library.

Published by:

Kaplan Publishing UK
Unit 2 The Business Centre
Molly Millars Lane
Wokingham
RG41 2QZ

ISBN 978-0-85732-776-5

© Kaplan Financial Limited, 2012

Printed and bound in Great Britain.

The text in this material and any others made available by any Kaplan Group company does not amount to advice on a particular matter and should not be taken as such. No reliance should be placed on the content as the basis for any investment or other decision or in connection with any advice given to third parties. Please consult your appropriate professional adviser as necessary. Kaplan Publishing Limited and all other Kaplan group companies expressly disclaim all liability to any person in respect of any losses or other claims, whether direct, indirect, incidental, consequential or otherwise arising in relation to the use of such materials.

CONTENTS

INTRODUCTION

STUDY TEXT

This study text has been specially prepared for the Institute of Certified Bookkeepers Computerised Bookkeeping II qualification.

It uses a case study approach to guide you through the syllabus and builds up your knowledge and skills chapter by chapter. The text is based upon Sage Instant Account V17, but can also be followed if you are using Sage Line 50 or other versions of Sage Instant Accounts.

Syllabus

This study text covers the entire syllabus below.

You must be able to demonstrate their ability to understand and carry out the following functions:

Business set up

(1)   Access the software

(2)   Set up the details of the new business including:

  (i)   Name, address, start up date, VAT registration where applicable,

  (ii)   Product lines for sale

  (iii)   Appropriate VAT rates

(3)   Set up customers' and suppliers' accounts in the sales and purchases ledger, with details of name, address, credit limit, opening balances where appropriate

(4)   Obtain a print out of all details in an appropriate and readable format

(5)   Set up appropriate accounts to record income and expenditure items

(6)   Set a pro-forma for the production of invoices, credit notes and other required documents

Ledger accounts

Make correct entries in the appropriate accounts for:

(1)   credit sales and purchases (including trade and cash discount where appropriate, individually or in batches)

(2)   credit notes sent to customers and received from suppliers

(3)   invoices received from suppliers for goods and services other than those for re-sale

(4)   cash sales and cash purchases

(5)   payments made on invoices received

(6)   receipts from invoices sent

(7)   payment of expenses and income other than from the sale of goods

(8)   transactions via the journal

(9)   Writing off of bad debts

Correction of errors

Correct any errors made in the posting of transactions to the accounts

Bank reconciliation

Carry out a bank reconciliation exercise using a computerised accounts package

Health and safety

Display an awareness of health and safety issues when using a computer system

Trial balances

(1)   Explain why they are needed

(2)   Explain the types of error that they will/will not disclose

(3)   Prepare such balances

(4)   Explain the action to be taken in the case of non-agreement

Reports

Print out required and explain the importance of reports including

(i)   audit trail

(ii)   nominal account transactions

(iii)   sales and purchases ledger transactions

(iv)   VAT returns

Final accounts of a sole trader

Extract a trading, profit and loss account and a balance sheet making allowances for year end adjustments such as depreciation (straight line and reducing balance methods), prepayments and accruals.

THE ASSESSMENT

The format of the assessment

The assessment takes the form of an online examination which can be sat at home, and relevant print-outs sent to the ICB for assessment. You will need to contact the ICB to register for this exam. You must have your own accounting software package.

Any accounting software package can be used but Microsoft Excel and other spreadsheets are not appropriate. The ICB advise students to exercise caution when using any software trial versions as they may offer restricted functionality, for example, a standard Sage trial version does not permit the user to print out the requisite reports.

Results are posted directly to the student within one calendar month of receipt of a completed answer paper.

If an examination is not returned within the deadline period, the examination will be graded as a Fail and the student must apply for a new examination and pay any necessary fees

The assessment itself takes the form of a case study approach of a fictional company. You will be asked to process transactions for this business, make corrections, and print out various reports for submission to the ICB. The practice assessment at the back of this study text will give you a very good understanding of what will be expected of you in the real examination. It is also strongly recommended you purchase an extra mock examination from the ICB's website as this will closely resemble the format of the real assessment.

STUDY SKILLS

Preparing to study

Devise a study plan

Determine which times of the week you will study.

Split these times into sessions of at least one hour for study of new material. Any shorter periods could be used for revision or practice.

Put the times you plan to study onto a study plan for the weeks from now until the assessment and set yourself targets for each period of study – in your sessions make sure you cover the whole course, activities and the associated questions in the workbook at the back of the manual.

If you are studying more than one qualification at a time, try to vary your subjects as this can help to keep you interested and see subjects as part of wider knowledge.

When working through your course, compare your progress with your plan and, if necessary, re-plan your work (perhaps including extra sessions) or, if you are ahead, do some extra revision / practice questions.

Effective studying

Active reading

You are not expected to learn the text by rote, rather, you must understand what you are reading and be able to use it to pass the assessment and develop good practice.

A good technique is to use SQ3Rs – Survey, Question, Read, Recall, Review:

1   **Survey the chapter**

    Look at the headings and read the introduction, knowledge, skills and content, so as to get an overview of what the chapter deals with.

2   **Question**

    Whilst undertaking the survey ask yourself the questions you hope the chapter will answer for you.

3   **Read**

Read through the chapter thoroughly working through the activities and, at the end, making sure that you can meet the learning objectives highlighted on the first page.

4   **Recall**

At the end of each section and at the end of the chapter, try to recall the main ideas of the section / chapter without referring to the text. This is best done after short break of a couple of minutes after the reading stage.

5   **Review**

Check that your recall notes are correct.

You may also find it helpful to re-read the chapter to try and see the topic(s) it deals with as a whole.

Note taking

Taking notes is a useful way of learning, but do not simply copy out the text.

The notes must:

- be in your own words
- be concise
- cover the key points
- well organised
- be modified as you study further chapters in this text or in related ones.

Trying to summarise a chapter without referring to the text can be a useful way of determining which areas you know and which you don't.

Three ways of taking notes

1   **Summarise the key points of a chapter**

2   **Make linear notes**

A list of headings, subdivided with sub-headings listing the key points.

If you use linear notes, you can use different colours to highlight key points and keep topic areas together.

Use plenty of space to make your notes easy to use.

3   Try a diagrammatic form

The most common of which is a mind map.

To make a mind map, put the main heading in the centre of the paper and put a circle around it.]

Draw lines radiating from this to the main sub-headings which again have circles around them.

Continue the process from the sub-headings to sub-sub-headings.

Highlighting and underlining

You may find it useful to underline or highlight key points in your study text – but do be selective.

You may also wish to make notes in the margins.

Further reading

In addition to this text, you should also read all the information contained within the ICB's examination area. It is strongly recommended you purchase an extra mock examination from the ICB's website.

KAPLAN PUBLISHING

An introduction to computerised bookkeeping

1

CONTENTS

1 Introduction

The aim of this manual is to guide you through the computerised accounting aspects of your studies.

To complete this manual you will need an understanding of the basics of double entry bookkeeping and a copy of SAGE. There are a number of versions of SAGE; this manual uses SAGE Instant Accounts version 17. If you have another version of SAGE, or even another accounting package, you should still be able to proceed without too much difficulty, although you may find that some of the screen-shots used in the manual differ.

The manual uses a case study approach to guide you step-by-step. It assumes that you have never used a computerised accounting package before. Even if you have, it is worth starting at the beginning to ensure that you don't 'jump ahead' too quickly.

2 Manual and computerised bookkeeping

The double entry system of bookkeeping that is still used today was developed in Italy in the fifteenth century. With the introduction of affordable and reliable information technology in the last thirty years, it was perhaps inevitable that business organisations would look to find ways to computerise their bookkeeping systems. Now it is rare to find an organisation which does not use some form of computer to aid in the day-to-day record keeping that is an essential aspect of running a business, whether large or small.

For very small organisations, a simple spreadsheet to record monies in and out of the business may suffice. However, once a business becomes larger or more complex, it may be beneficial to introduce a computerised bookkeeping system. There are many proprietary versions on the market, each of which works in a similar way but which will offer different approaches to data entry, presentation of reports and so on, as well as different 'extras' such as stock management modules, budgeting and tax planning. Some systems also allow a company to integrate a computerised payroll function.

3 Benefits of a computerised system

The main benefits ascribed to a computerised bookkeeping system are:

- Quicker, more efficient processing of data

- Fewer mathematical errors – because the system completes all the double entry and other mathematical functions (e.g. calculation of percentages) there is reduced opportunity for human error

- Accounting documents (e.g. invoices, statements etc) can be generated automatically, using tailored documents designed to incorporate company details, logos etc

- The range of information that can be easily produced in reports is wide and varied, meaning businesses can report to various internal and external groups (e.g. management, directors, shareholders, banks etc) in an appropriate format

- There is no need for manual processing of data – computerised bookkeeping systems complete all the double entry automatically

- Hardware and software prices have fallen dramatically over the last thirty years, making a computerised system affordable to all organisations

- Data may be easily transferred into other programs – e.g. a spreadsheet or word processing package

4 Accounting documents

Business organisations rely on relevant documentation to record the transactions that they undertake. Without an appropriate piece of supporting documentation, there is no way of knowing what has been bought, from whom and for how much, nor indeed what has been sold. With a high proportion of modern transactions being on credit, an accurate and comprehensive system of recording transactions is essential.

Many business documents are referred to as 'Primary Records'. They include:

- purchase orders

- delivery notes

- purchase invoices

- sales invoices
- debit notes
- credit notes

These documents are used to record business transactions in the first instance. For example, if an organisation wishes to purchase a new computer printer, it may first raise a purchase order which is sent to the supplier. The supplier would issue or deliver the printer along with a delivery note, to record the safe receipt of the goods. A supplier invoice requiring payment would follow. If the printer was faulty, it could be returned and a credit note issued.

In order for a transaction to be correctly recorded in a computerised accounting system, the appropriate documentation must first be raised and then the details entered into 'the system'; indeed, many organisations employ accounting staff whose job is primarily to enter the data accurately and completely from the source documents.

There are many other documents which are also essential in maintaining an up-to-date and accurate accounting system. Bank statements, schedules of direct debits/standing orders, supplier statements, correspondence from suppliers and customers and so on also provide invaluable information which can be used to check the computerised bookkeeping system for accuracy.

In the course of the case study which follows, you will be required to enter details from a range of source documents, and use other documents, to maintain a computerised bookkeeping system for a small company.

KAPLAN PUBLISHING

5 Retention of documents

There are legal requirements for businesses to retain source documents beyond the end of the accounting period to which they relate. The Limitations Act 1980 deals with this issue in general; however, there are many other pieces of specific legislation which place a responsibility on businesses to retain their records.

Accounting and Banking Records	
Ledgers, invoices, cheques, paying-in documents, bank statements and standing order instructions	Must all be retained for a minimum of six years
Employee Records	
All personnel records	6 years from end of employment
Senior Executive personnel records	Permanently
Rejected job applications	One year
Time cards, payroll records and expenses claims	Six years
Medical records and accident records	Permanently
Contractual Arrangements	
Simple contracts – e.g. with suppliers or customers	6 years after expiration of contract
Contracts relating to land and buildings	12 years after expiration of contract
Trust deeds (e.g. mortgages)	Permanently
Statutory Returns and Records of Board Meetings	
All statutory returns (e.g. to Companies House)	Permanently
Notices, circulars and minutes of board meetings	Permanently

Safe retention of records such as these is important not only to fulfil an organisation's legal obligations, but also because they may prove an invaluable source of reference – for example in a future complaint against a supplier.

However, all organisations must ensure that these documents are stored in such a way that they are easily accessible if required, kept secure from unauthorised access, and kept safe from physical damage (e.g. water or fire damage).

6 Coding

Most computerised bookkeeping systems work by the use of codes. Each supplier and each customer must be given a unique code by which the computer software can recognise them. It is vital that there can be no confusion between two suppliers with similar names. For example, you may be fully aware that John Green and John Greenwood are entirely different people, but it could be easy for a computer to mix them up. Each must therefore be given a unique code by which they can be identified.

Similarly, each product manufactured or sold by an organisation may be given a unique code. Employees, also, are usually 'coded' – you could check your pay slip to find your own Employee Reference Number.

Finally, every type of income or expense, asset or liability, is given a unique code to identify it. This makes entering transactions quite straightforward, since you need only refer to the relevant four digit code rather than a long narrative description.

Codes must be unique. However, they should also be recognisable by the person dealing with the system. For example, if a supplier was coded "SMITH006", this would be far more recognisable than a purely numeric code such as "0827329".

Care must be taken to issue codes that are not ambiguous. The use of a combination of letters and numbers (an alphanumeric code) often achieves this.

In SAGE, when you create a new customer or supplier record, the program will automatically suggest a code for that supplier. It does this by taking the first eight characters of the name. The suggested code for a customer called Greenwood would therefore be "GREENWOO". You may decide this is not the most appropriate code (think what the problem might be if you had two different suppliers called Greenwood), in which case you can easily change it. Many organisations have a set structure for coding, and if this is the case in your organisation you should follow it.

Installing SAGE for the first time

CONTENTS
1   Installing SAGE

1 Installing SAGE

When you load SAGE v17 for the first time you should see the following screen:

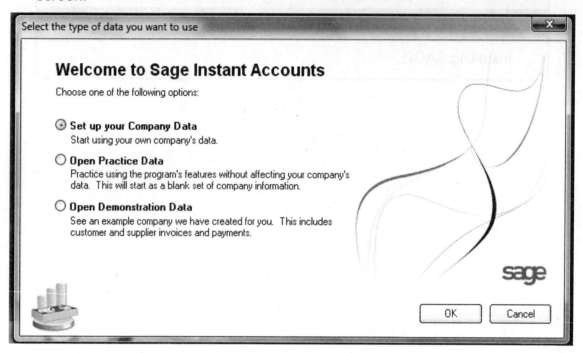

Select the type of data you want to use

Welcome to Sage Instant Accounts

Choose one of the following options:

⊙ **Set up your Company Data**
Start using your own company's data.

○ **Open Practice Data**
Practice using the program's features without affecting your company's data. This will start as a blank set of company information.

○ **Open Demonstration Data**
See an example company we have created for you. This includes customer and supplier invoices and payments.

sage

OK   Cancel

Assuming you are entering a new company (as you will be doing here, make sure that the "set up your company data" is marked. Don't worry at this stage about the other options – just press the [OK] button.

You should now see this screen:

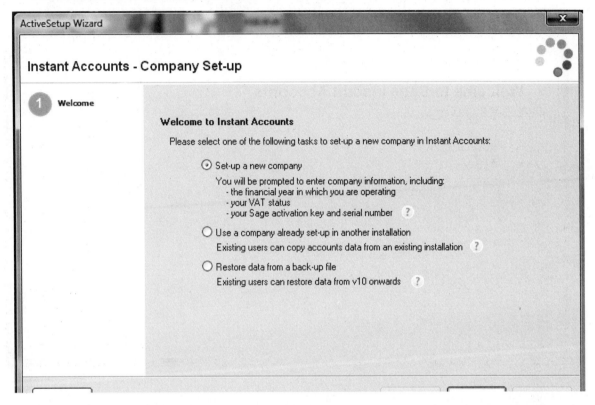

Your choice here depends on whether you are setting up a new company, or uploading existing data.

For now, you will be starting with a completely new company, so click on the "SET UP A NEW COMPANY" button as shown.

Once you have company details set up and saved in SAGE, it will default to that company each time you start up.

KAPLAN PUBLISHING

Setting up your company

3

CONTENTS

1   Background to the company
2   Setting up the company

1 Background to the company

Wynn Bowlden is a self-employed tennis coach who operates as a sole trader. She coaches a range of clients from around the county of Mellinghamshire.

She rents a small office above a sports shop in the market town of Pickerton from which she conducts her business. As well as coaching her clients she also sells a range of tennis clothing and equipment which she obtains from a number of UK-based suppliers.

Wynn has asked you to help her with her bookkeeping. She currently uses a manual bookkeeping system. However, she now feels that the business has grown sufficiently to justify using a computerised accounting package, since she needs more timely and accurate financial information on which to base decisions about the business.

Today's date is 31st December 2011 – the last day of the business's financial year.

2 Setting up the company

Introduction

When you start using SAGE for your company you must firstly enter some information about the company itself. This is important because it will identify this particular company and appear on various reports. In addition, at this stage, you must enter the start dates of the company's financial year. This is vitally important, as SAGE will use this information in producing your annual accounts.

Data

You will need the following information for this session.

Business Name:	Wynn Bowlden Tennis Coach
Business Address:	15 Love Street
	Pickerton
	Mellinghamshire
	ML40 3TT
Telephone:	01989 2891891
Fax:	01989 2891891
Email:	info@wynnbowlden.webnet.uk
Website:	www.wynnbowlden.co.uk
VAT Number:	734 9281 07
Financial Year:	1st January – 31st December

Now we can begin entering the data for our business.

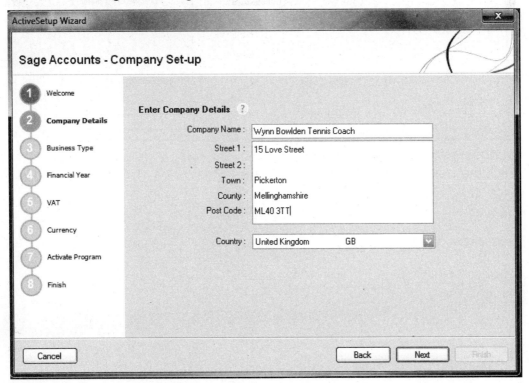

Be sure to check for accuracy – but don't worry if you make a mistake because you can always amend it later. Once you are happy with your entries click on the | Next | button.

Step One – Selecting the business type

On this screen you can choose a business type for your business, this amends the nominal codes so they are specific for your business. These are reference numbers by which we will refer to different types of asset, liability, income and expense as you start to enter transactions. You will learn more about nominal codes in Chapter 8. For this exercise we are going to select the General (standard) type.

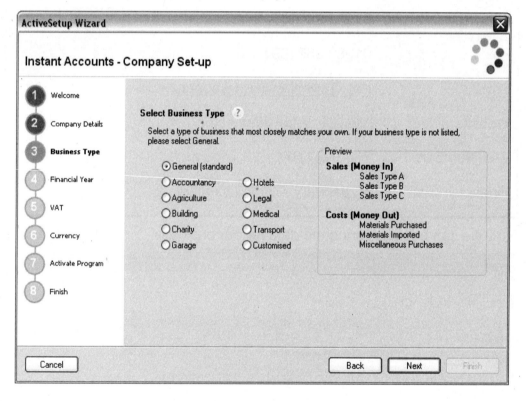

Click the next button | Next |.

Step Two – Entering the details of the Financial Year

This is a really important stage. You need to enter the dates of your company's Financial Year. Remember, for Wynn Bowldon the business's Financial Year is 1st January 2011 – 31st December 2011.

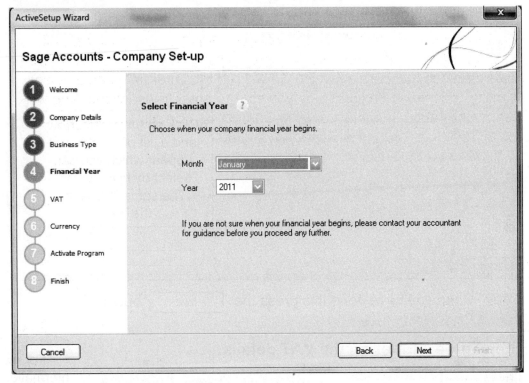

The data in this manual all refers to the year 2011, and so our Financial Year will start in **January 2011**. Enter this, using the drop down boxes.

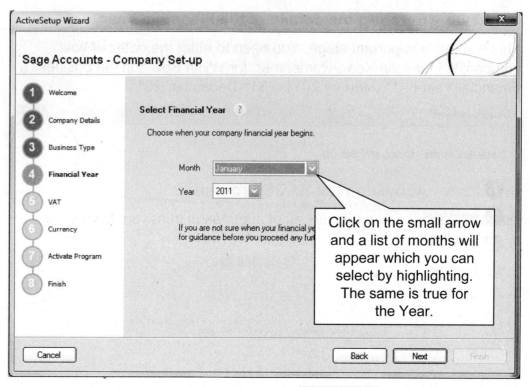

Again, when you have done this press the [Next] button.

Step Three – Entering the VAT details

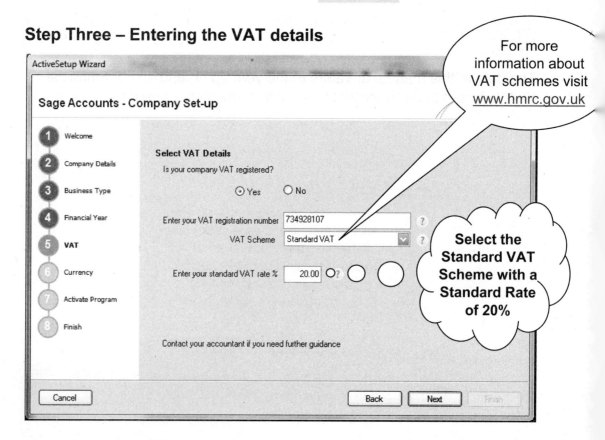

Step Four – Entering the currency details

At this stage you can enter the currency details. All of Wynn Bowlden's transactions take place in the UK, and so their base currency is "Pound Sterling".

You should check that this option is correctly checked.

Again, click the [Next] button to proceed.

Step Five – Activating the SAGE program

You now need to enter two pieces of information from your SAGE box. You need both the Serial Number and the Activation Key to proceed.

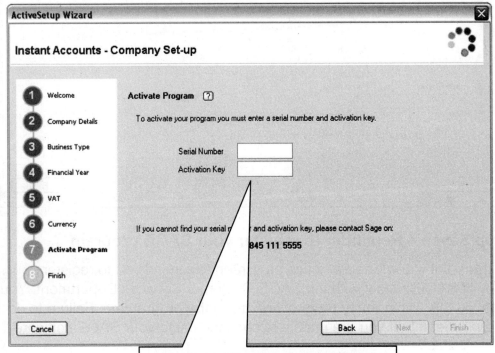

The Serial Number and Activation Key can be found on a sticky label labelled "Important Information" inside your SAGE box. These are unique numbers which help to prevent fraudulent use of the software. These are important, and you must keep them in a safe place!

Step Six – Active Setup

Well done – you have now set up SAGE with the basic information needed for the business. At this stage you can simply press the [Finish] button to move to the next stage.

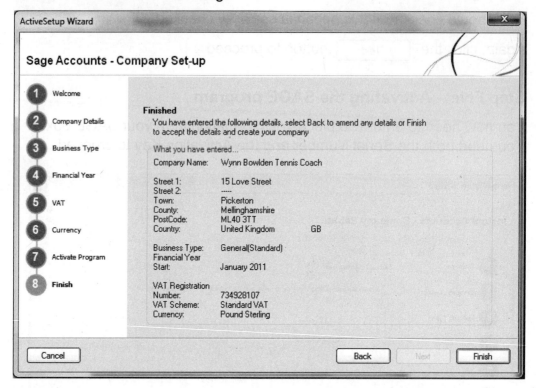

Step Seven – Reminder to register your SAGE program

At this point you will see a notice on screen to remind you to register your copy of SAGE Instant with the SAGE Customer Services Department. You must do this within **thirty days** of first using the programme. Failure to do this will mean that you are unable to continue using your SAGE software.

Click [OK] to continue.

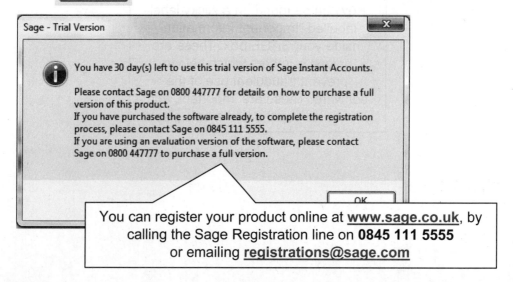

You can register your product online at **www.sage.co.uk**, by calling the Sage Registration line on **0845 111 5555** or emailing **registrations@sage.com**

You will now be given information regarding how to obtain SAGE Updates. Please read these carefully and proceed as you wish.

The first screen (or 'window') you will then see is shown below:

Take time to become familiar with the different options on this screen – you are unlikely to use all of them (at least to begin with), but it is good to explore them at this stage. When you are ready to move on to the next Chapter, click on the ‎Customers‎ tab from the panel on the lower left hand side of the screen.

Navigating SAGE

CONTENTS

1 Introduction

You have by now opened your SAGE Instant software and set up the basic details of the business. The next stage is to check your business data and then to practice navigating your way around the different sections of SAGE. Don't worry if you have never used a package like SAGE before – so long as you can use a mouse you will be fine.

This 'window' (or screen) is the one that will now appear every time you open SAGE Instant. You will explore it in more detail as you progress through the manual. For now, just take the time to familiarise yourself with this screen. Make sure you maximise the screen.

If you can't see the Links Panel simply place your cursor on the line and drag it upwards to expose the panel.

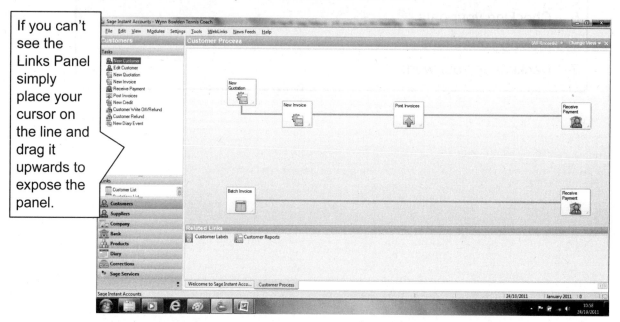

This screen enables you to access a range of accounting activities connected with your customers. You can:

1   Produce a new quotation for a potential customer.

2   Create an invoice to send or give to a customer.

3   Post (enter) the details of that invoice onto SAGE.

4   Receive and account for a payment made by a customer.

Note that you can access each of these activities in a number of ways.

The easiest are via:

(a)   The *RELATED LINKS TABS* at the bottom of the screen

(b)   The options on the *TASKS PANEL*

(c)   The options on the *LINKS PANEL*

(d)   The icons on the *CUSTOMER PROCESS* screen

You will practice each of these later on in this manual.

Of course, every business needs customers, but they are not the only aspect of a business. Any business will also need suppliers (of goods, raw materials and services). It will then also need to keep a record of the stock that it carries – whether of raw materials, work in progress or finished goods for sale. It will need a bank account (or maybe more than one!) in which to place its receipts and from which to make payments. SAGE also allows you to input accounting activities with each of these.

It is very simple to access the different parts of SAGE.

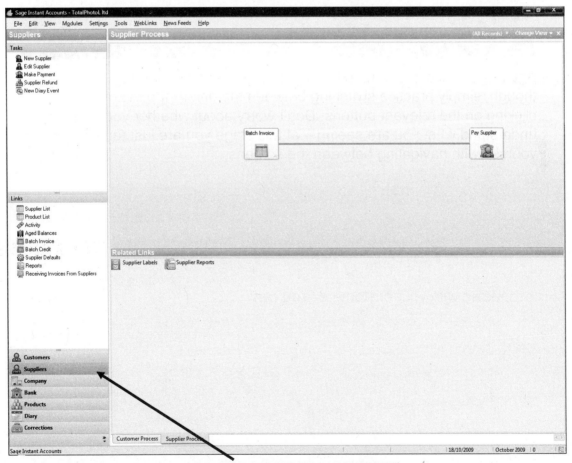

To begin with, click on

This will bring up a new window with a different series of icons.

2 The supplier process screen

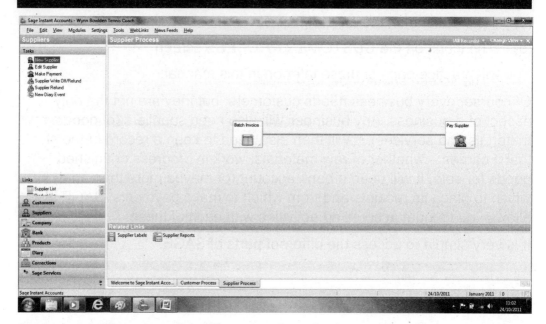

Again, you will explore the different options in due course. For now, though, simply practice switching between the different parts of SAGE by clicking on the relevant buttons. Don't worry about whether you can understand what you are seeing – at this stage you are just familiarising yourself with navigating between the screens.

Exercise

Start at the Customer Process Screen.

Navigate to the following screens:

❶   Suppliers ⇨ Pay Supplier (looks like 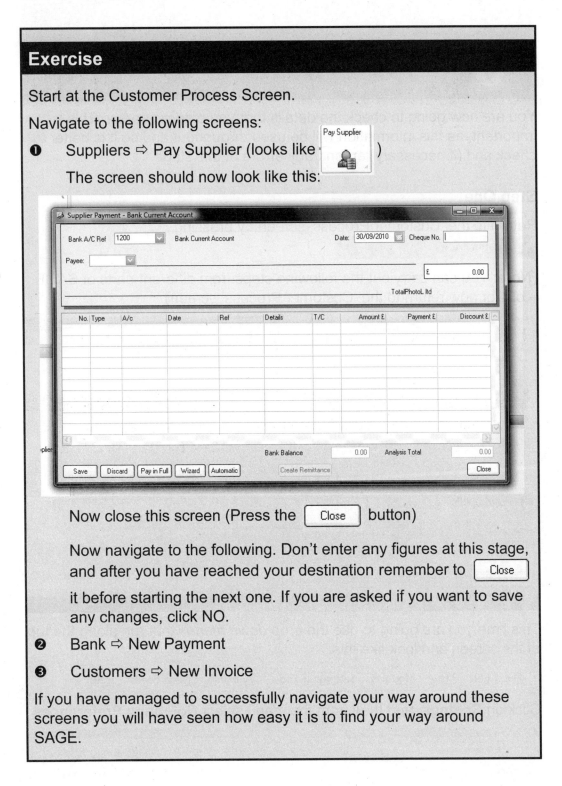)

The screen should now look like this:

Now close this screen (Press the | Close | button)

Now navigate to the following. Don't enter any figures at this stage, and after you have reached your destination remember to | Close |

it before starting the next one. If you are asked if you want to save any changes, click NO.

❷   Bank ⇨ New Payment

❸   Customers ⇨ New Invoice

If you have managed to successfully navigate your way around these screens you will have seen how easy it is to find your way around SAGE.

3 Checking your company details

You are now going to check the details that you entered earlier. This is important, as this information will be used throughout and so it is better to check and (if necessary) amend any errors at this stage.

Step One

Return to the 'Customer Process' screen by pressing

(**Note:** You can carry out the following steps from different parts of SAGE – but for now return to the 'Customer Process' screen)

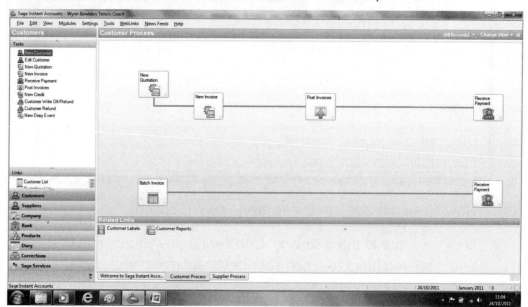

This time you are going to use the *drop down menus* that run along the top of the screen and look like this.

Click on **Settings,** and then from the menu select **Company Preferences.**

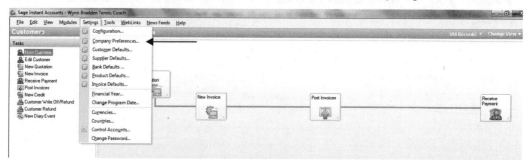

You will now be warned that all other sections of SAGE must be closed down before you can examine these company details. Make sure that you have done this and click the Yes button.

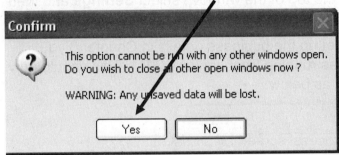

You should not have any data in any other sections at this point, and so you need not worry about losing it.

You will now see the company details that you input earlier. You should now thoroughly check these to make sure that they are correct.

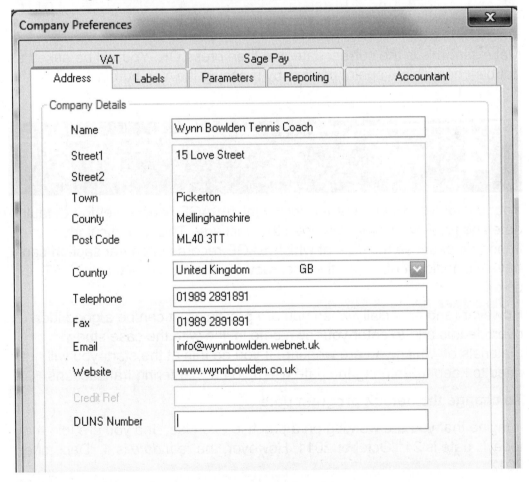

You can now check the information you entered about the financial year is also correct.

Again using the *menus* at the top of the window, select **Settings** and then **Financial Year.**

REMEMBER – when we set up the business details in Chapter 3 you entered the financial year as running from January 2011. This should now be showing on the screen, as below.

Make sure this is the correct date and then press OK. You will be asked to double-check this – again, confirm by pressing the Yes button.

4 Dates

Your computer has an internal clock, which SAGE uses to set the default date and time every time you open the package. This is particularly important because the date at which SAGE records each transaction can have a significant effect on the accuracy of reports, calculation of VAT and so on.

However (and especially when you are practising) it can be a good idea to override this and to enter your own date in line with the case study materials on which you are working. If you do this at the start, you will not need to keep re-entering the date when you are entering transactions.

To change the default program date

Imagine that you are working on a practise exercise, and you are told that today's date is 24th October 2011. However, the *real date* is 4th December 2012.

The default date in SAGE for entering transactions will show as 4th December – and you would have to override this each and every time you made an entry. This is repetitive and increases the likelihood of making a mistake – entering "05" instead of "04", for example.

Fortunately SAGE allows you to change the default date. Simply select the SETTINGS menu, and then CHANGE PROGRAM DATE.

Now you can easily change the date that required by the assessment material – in this case 24th October 2011. Now, every time you enter a transaction in SAGE the date will default to 24th October. This will have no effect on your computer's internal clock, and the next time you use the program the default date will revert to the real date once more until you change it.

Task

In the Wynn Bowlden Case Study, you are told that today's date is 31st December 2011. You should now change the SAGE program date on your computer to 31st December 2011. Remember that if you subsequently shut SAGE down, when you return to it you will need to change the default date again.

5 Checking your data

If you work steadily and carefully, you should not encounter many problems with your data entry. However, no matter how carefully you work, you will undoubtedly have to make corrections at some time – either because of human error in inputting data, or simply because new information comes to light.

One important feature of SAGE is the ability to check your data. This will help to identify any issues with data corruption (which can occur after a power cut, for example), missing data and date errors.

You can access the DataCheck facility by clicking on FILE in the main menu bar, then MAINTENANCE, and then CHECK DATA.

SAGE will check the validity of your data and advise you of any possible discrepancies.

You should note that the DataCheck facility will <u>not</u> identify data entry errors (e.g. entering the wrong amount or posting to the wrong nominal code). The accuracy of data entry is your responsibility, and you should therefore aim to minimise the number of errors you make by being careful to check your work at all stages.

6 Making corrections

Many people are understandably a little nervous when using a computer system for the first time. They worry that they may break the system, or make mistakes that cannot be corrected.

Don't worry: SAGE offers a number of easy ways to amend or wipe errors.

These are covered in more detail later, but for now let us look at one of the more common mistakes that you may make – the simple (but frustrating!) entry of an incorrect figure.

 Example

Imagine you are entering a purchase of some stationery for £10.00. In error, you enter £100.00, and post the transaction into the system before you notice your mistake. What should you do?

To start with, don't panic!

One of the great advantages of a computerised system is that most errors are easy to correct. In SAGE, many amendments are carried out using the MAINTENANCE – CORRECTIONS function.

Click on FILE in the main menu bar, then on MAINTENANCE, and finally CORRECTIONS.

You will now see a list of all the transactions you have entered in chronological order which can be amended

You now have two choices; you can either AMEND a previously-entered transaction, or DELETE it completely.

In the example above, you would simply want to amend the transaction. You could choose to amend the purchaser or supplier code, the product description, or the reference and date. In order to change other aspects of the transaction, such as the nominal code, the amounts or the VAT rate, you should click on the EDIT button.

It is relatively straightforward to correct most errors in this way; however, some errors require a different approach. These are covered in more detail later.

7 Backing up your work

It is important that you back up your data regularly, to guard against accidental losses which can prove very costly and time-consuming to recover or re-input.

Backing up your data should become part of your daily routine.

From the File menu at the top of the screen select 'Backup'.

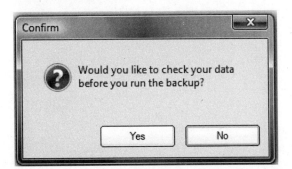

SAGE now asks if you would like to check your data before you run the backup – you should select [Yes]

Hopefully there are no problems with your data files and so you will now be able to backup your data.

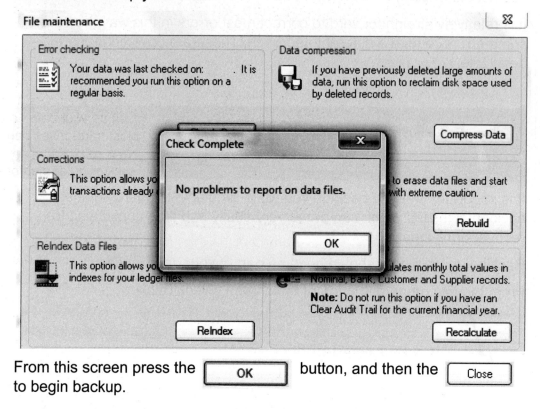

From this screen press the [OK] button, and then the [Close] to begin backup.

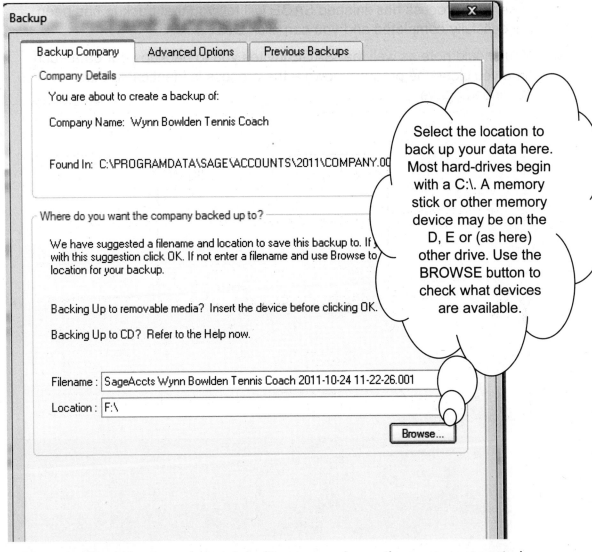

You need to select an appropriate file name – here, the name suggested by SAGE has been used but you could select another name to suit your own needs. Select **OK** to back up. The screen will now show a "Backup" box which indicates the progress of the backup.

When this process has finished SAGE will tell you that backup has been successfully completed and you can click **OK**.

You should note as well that SAGE invites you to backup your data each time you close the program down – the process is identical to that described above.

Setting up your suppliers' details

5

CONTENTS

1 Introduction

Most business organisations will, over time, deal with a wide range of suppliers. A café may have different suppliers for their meat, cheese, vegetables, wine etc. A hairdresser will buy different products from different suppliers. Sometimes supplies will be obtained from a *wholesaler* or a *cash and carry*; other supplies may be sourced directly from the *manufacturers.*

The organisation will need to keep very accurate and timely records of all transactions with their suppliers. These transactions will typically include:

(1)   Purchases and returns

(2)   Discounts received from the supplier

(3)   Payments made to the supplier in settlement of outstanding bills

In addition, it would be very convenient to have all the contact details of every supplier easily to hand.

Fortunately SAGE provides a very comprehensive Supplier management system which covers all these requirements (and more). You will see how this works shortly, but firstly you will need to enter your suppliers' details.

2 Supplier data

Wynn Bowlden has five suppliers, whose details are given below:

Yonnad Tenniswear Ltd   A/c Ref : YT001

30 Sampras Lane

Laver

Derbyshire

DB18 8HY

Tel 01829 389228

Contact: Holly Maclay

Outstanding Balance at 31st December 2011: **£864.10**

Credit Terms: **30 days, 2% 7 days**   Credit Limit **£2,500**

Kike Shoes Ltd   A/c Ref : KS001

40 Murray Street

Rosewall

North Yorkshire

YO18 8DV

Tel 0845 2381989

Contact: Emily WIlls

Outstanding Balance at 31st December 2011: **£1,208.19**

Credit Terms: **30 days, 2% 7 days**   Credit Limit **£2,500**

Wilkinson Tennis Balls Ltd   A/c Ref : WT003

30 Blake Avenue

Great Ashe

Somerset

SM18 6FG

Tel 0800 3898191

Contact: Emma Moore

Outstanding Balance at 31st December 2011: **£1529.10**

Credit Terms: **14 days, no settlement discount**   Credit Limit **£3,000**

Wotta Rackets Ltd   A/c Ref : WR002
30 Nadal Way
Little Evert
Edinburgh
ED17 3HP

Tel 0800 1902029

Contact: Ruby Catt

Outstanding Balance at 31st December 2011: **£209.34**

Credit Terms: **21 days, 1% 7 days**   **Credit Limit £1,000**

First Serve Office Supplies Ltd   A/c Ref : FS001
15 Venus Heights
Mottram
Devon
SW88 7BV

Tel 0845 8728382

Contact: Robin Holly

Outstanding Balance at 31st December 2011: **£401.35**

Credit Terms: **30 days, 2.5% 10 days**   **Credit Limit £2,500**

3 Entering supplier details

From the Supplier Process window (below) press the **New Supplier** task.

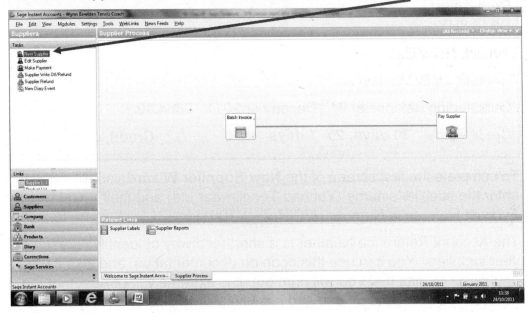

This will bring up the **Supplier Record Wizard**, which will help you to easily enter your suppliers' details.

To continue with this you will need to refer to the list of suppliers for Wynn Bowlden on the previous pages.

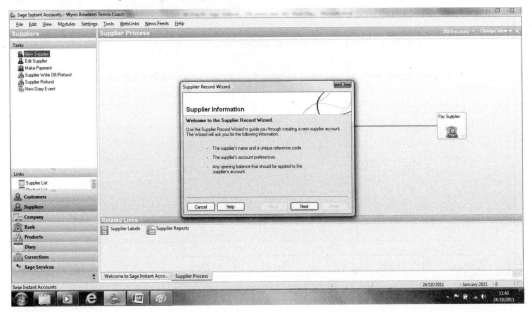

The first supplier to enter from page 37 is:

Yonnad Tenniswear Ltd   A/c Ref : YT001
30 Sampras Lane
Laver
Derbyshire
DB18 8HY

Tel 01829 389228

Contact: Holly Maclay

Outstanding Balance at 31st December 2011: **£864.10**

Credit Terms: **30 days, 2% 7 days**   **Credit Limit £2,500**

To complete the first screen of the **New Supplier Wizard** you will need to enter the supplier's name (Yonnad Tenniswear Ltd) and their unique Account Reference Number (A/C Ref – YT001).

The Account Reference Number is a shorthand way of identifying each of your suppliers. You can use this code on documentation, and also it will appear on reports that you will print out. It is extremely important that the number you choose is unique and it is useful if it helps to identify the supplier in some way – here YT001 representing **Y**onnad **T**enniswear.

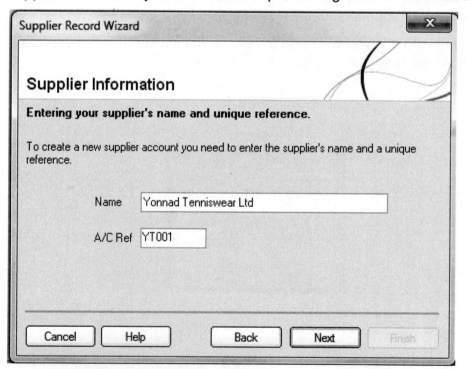

It is important to check your spelling for accuracy as errors (although they can be rectified) can cause confusion. In particular, ensure you use the correct account code (YT001) as this *cannot* subsequently be changed.

If you are happy press the [Next] button to move on. You will now need to enter the supplier's address, telephone and (if you have them) fax details. Again, when you are happy, press the [Next] button.

Now you can enter the firm's contact details. In this case we have not got an e-mail or website address, or the VAT number. Don't worry, though, as these can easily be entered at a later date. You can enter Holly Maclay's name at this point, though, before pressing the [Next] button.

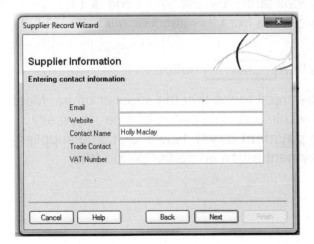

The next screen asks you to enter details of your credit terms with this supplier, the nominal code against which purchases from this supplier will be recorded, and also the most common VAT rating for the goods that you buy from them.

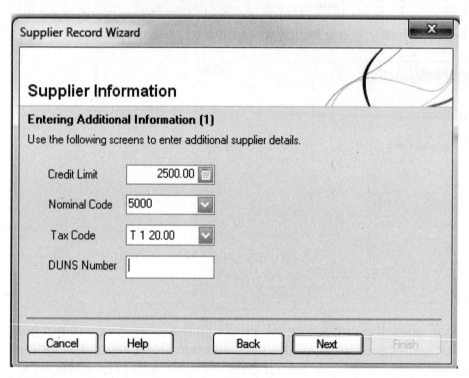

Here we can enter the credit limit of £2500. The nominal code is 5000 (you will learn more about nominal codes later) and the VAT code is T1, meaning that the majority of purchases from this supplier will have VAT added at 20.0%.

If you are happy with this press the [Next] button.

Now you can enter details of any credit terms that the supplier offers. Most suppliers will insist on payment within a certain period of time – typically seven to twenty eight days **(the payment days).** However, some suppliers may also offer a discount for payment within an earlier period **(the settlement days)**.

Yonnad Tenniswear Ltd offer credit terms of **"2% 7days"** meaning that if Wynn Bowlden settles invoices within 7 days she can deduct a 2% discount from the amount owing. This needs to be reflected in the next window as shown below.

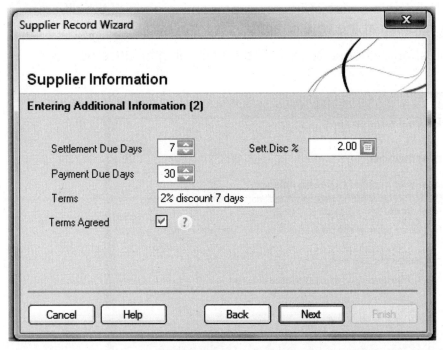

You will also want to tick the terms agreed box, as this tells Sage that the details have been confirmed.

The next screens ask you to enter the details of your supplier's bank. This is essential if you will be paying the supplier using methods such as BACS. It is not necessary if you will always be paying by cheque.

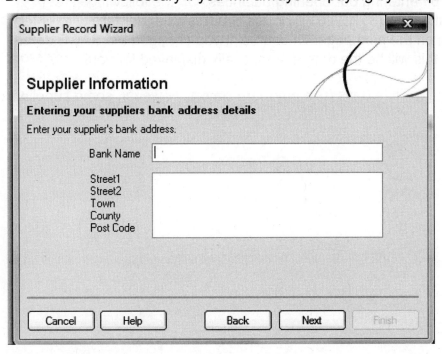

SAGE now asks if this supplier has an outstanding balance – in other words, if at the time of entering their details you already owe them money. In this example, Wynn Bowlden currently owes Yonnad Tenniswear Ltd £864.10. This figure can be entered either as one figure, or alternatively could be entered as a series of figures representing each of the different outstanding invoices at the time of entry.

For now, you should choose to enter the outstanding balance as one figure.

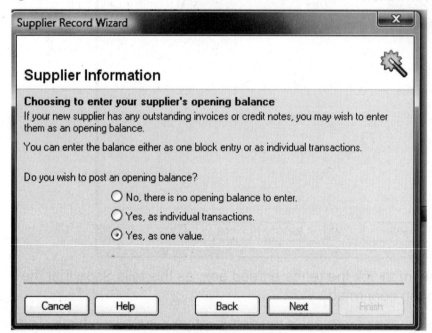

Remember today's date is 31st December 2011. This is therefore the date that we will be entering our opening balances. On the following screen either type the date (31/12/2011) or use SAGE's calendar facility to enter it, as shown on the next page. Of course, if you changed the SAGE default date earlier this will be the date automatically displayed for you!

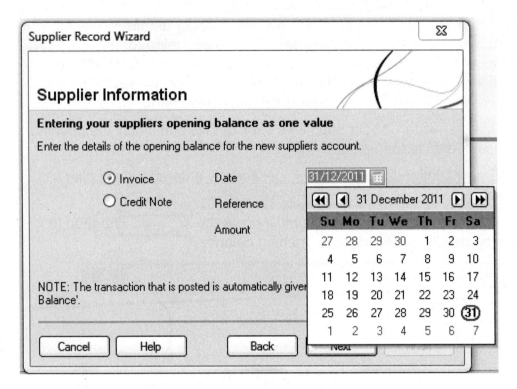

You can now enter the opening balance for Yonnad Tenniswear Ltd. Check your entries then press the [Next] button.

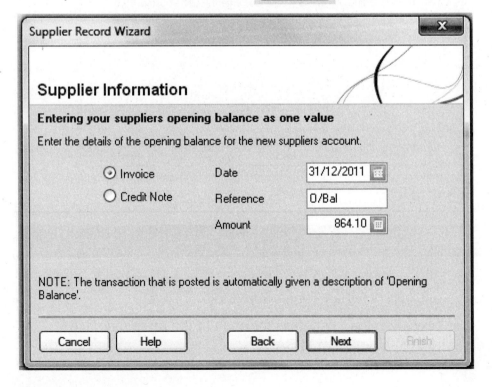

Well done! You have now entered your first supplier details. To recap, you began by entering their company details, such as their address, phone and fax numbers and contact details. Then you entered the credit terms that this supplier makes available to us, including normal payment terms and any discounts that are available for early settlement.

After that you entered your supplier's bank details and finally the opening balance of debt to that supplier.

SAGE now confirms that you have successfully entered the supplier's details.

The next stage is important – you *must* press the [Finish] button to save the details and to post the opening balance.

Exercise

Refer back to pages 37 and 38. You have already entered one of Wynn Bowlden's suppliers (Yonnad Tenniswear Ltd).

You should now enter the full details for each of the remaining five suppliers, and then save them to SAGE.

4 Entering detailed invoices or nil balances

When you entered the opening balances for Wynn Bowlden's suppliers, you simply entered them as one amount. In reality, of course, these opening balances are likely to be made up of a number of different outstanding invoices, along perhaps with one or more credit notes. If this is the case, it would be useful to record each outstanding invoice separately, so that it can be referred to when payment is eventually received. In order to do this, you would simply click the button labelled "Yes, as individual transactions".

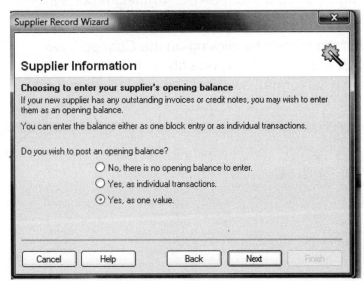

You will now be able to enter each outstanding invoice or credit note individually.

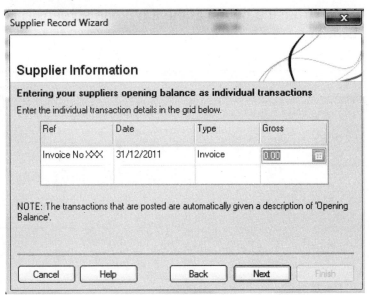

Entering Zero Balances

Sometimes an existing supplier will have no outstanding invoices at the date they are entered into the system. In this situation, simply click on the "No, there is no opening balance to enter" button.

5 Printing supplier data reports

You have entered the details of the five suppliers, so let's now check that they are correct by running off a report from SAGE. Printing reports in SAGE is straightforward, using the Report Browser Function.

Firstly, change the View of the screen by clicking on the Change View dropdown menu and select Suppliers. This presents all the suppliers that you have entered so far in a list format, as shown below, including their outstanding balances.

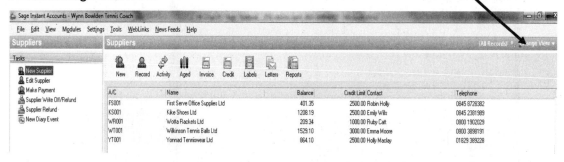

Now select the Reports icon from the ribbon at the top of the screen. This will launch the Reports Browser.

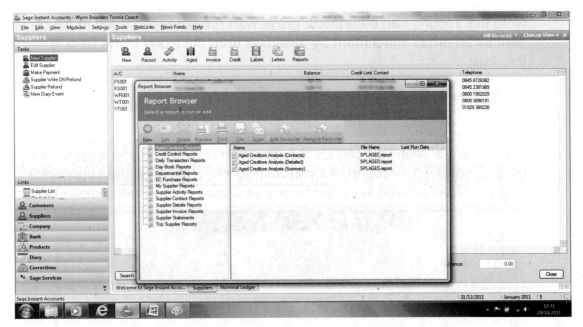

This will produce a new window with a list of supplier-related reports that you could want to print and use. You will practice accessing some more of these later on, but for now the one that you want is the report entitled *Supplier Address List*. This is contained within the folder called *Supplier Details Reports* – to access the contents of this (or any) folder simply double click on it.

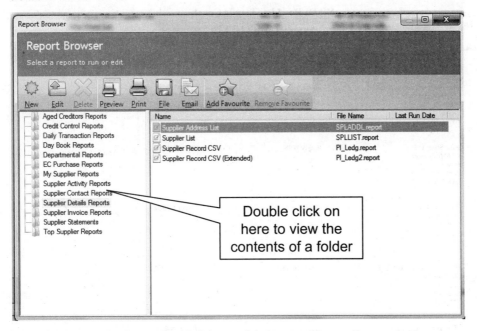

Double click on *Supplier Address List* to produce the report.

Note that reports can be printed, previewed (on screen), saved to file or sent as an email attachment by selecting from the icons in the Report Browser.

Preview   Print   File   Email

On the next screen you can identify the criteria by which you wish to select the contents of your report. As you wish to see a list of all the suppliers that you have entered keep the boxes as shown below, then press OK.

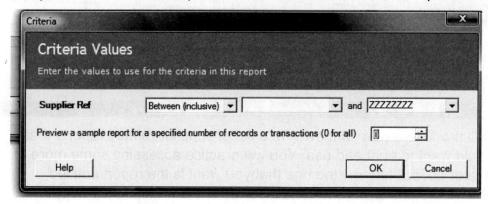

Your report should now show on screen, similar to the one below.

Date:	24/10/2011		**Wynn Bowlden Tennis Coach**		Page:	1
Time:	12:40:10		**Supplier Address List**			

Supplier From:					
Supplier To:	ZZZZZZZZ				

A/C	Name	Contact	Telephone	Fax
FS001	First Serve Office Supplies Ltd 15 Venus Heights Mottram Devon SW88 7BV	Robin Holly	0845 8728382	
KS001	Kike Shoes Ltd 40 Murray Street Rosewall North Yorkshire YO18 8DV	Emily Wills	0845 2381989	
WR001	Wotta Rackets Ltd 30 Nadal Way Little Evert Edinburgh ED17 3HP	Ruby Catt	0800 1902029	
WT001	Wilkinson Tennis Balls Ltd 30 Blake Avenue Great Ashe Somerset SM18 6FG	Emma Moore	0800 3898191	
YT001	Yonnad Tenniswear Ltd 30 Sampras Lane Laver Derbyshire DB18 8HY	Holly Maclay	01829 389228	

KAPLAN PUBLISHING

There are many other supplier reports available in this section – you should now feel confident enough to access these and to print them out. The exact list of reports that you will use will depend on your particular requirements, and you will see some of the more common ones later in this manual.

Setting up your customers' details

CONTENTS

1 Introduction
2 Customer data
3 Printing customer data reports

1 Introduction

Now that you have successfully entered your suppliers' details you can now move on to enter relevant information about your customers as well.

The process of entering your customers' details is very similar to that of entering supplier information, so you should feel confident doing this now.

It is of course vitally important that you keep accurate records for each of your customers. This information is likely to include:

(1) Sales made on credit to customers, and sales returns

(2) Credit terms for your customers, including any discount they may receive

(3) Contact details for easy invoicing

(4) Payments received from customers

Consistent, accurate recording of information is a vital aspect of any credit management system, ensuring that your organisation gets paid as quickly as possible for its sales. This can be the difference between failure and survival for most businesses.

2 Customer data

Wynn Bowlden has five customers with outstanding balances as at 30th September 2010. Their details are given below:

Roland Garros   A/c Ref : GAR001
10 Paris Boulevard
Hostleton
Mellinghamshire
HO97 6TF

Outstanding Balance at 31st December 2011: **£301.28**

Credit Terms: **Payment in 28 days**   **Credit Limit £500**

Rank Outsiders Ltd   A/c Ref : RAN002
No2 Court Trading Estate
Tarryton
Mellinghamshire
TY17 6DS

Outstanding Balance at 31st December 2011: **£1820.49**

Credit Terms: **Payment in 28 days**   **Credit Limit £5000**

Noah Chang   A/c Ref : CHA001
40 Love Street
Portshead
Mellinghamshire
PH28 5CV

Outstanding Balance at 31st December 2011: **£109.26**

Credit Terms: **Payment in 28 days**   **Credit Limit £500**

Little Smashers Junior Tennis Club

A/c Ref : LIT001

No 1 Sinceperry Avenue
Hurby
Mellinghamshire
HB80 9PL

Outstanding Balance at 31st December 2011: **£209.47**

Credit Terms: **Payment in 28 days**   **Credit Limit £1000**

Annette Chord

A/c Ref : CHO001

20 New York Street
Bridgeford
Mellinghamshire
BG16 9JY

Outstanding Balance at 31st December 2011: **£819.20**

Credit Terms: **Payment in 28 days**   **Credit Limit £1000**

You will now enter these five customer details into SAGE.

Step One

Go to the Customer Process screen, as below.

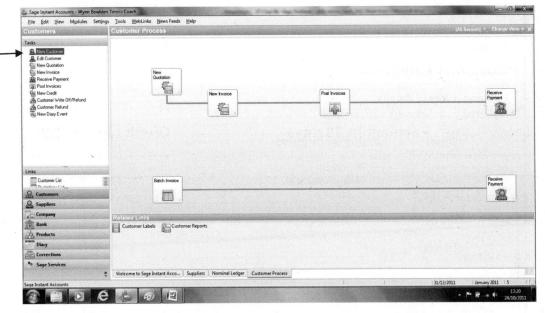

From the Task Bar, click on New Customer. At the next screen click NEXT, and you should now be able to enter your first customer's details, as below.

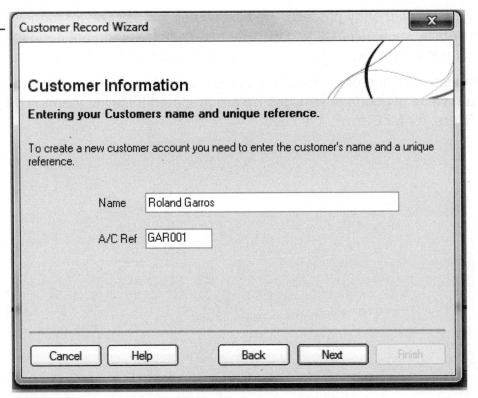

When you have done this click the NEXT button again, and enter the address details, as below.

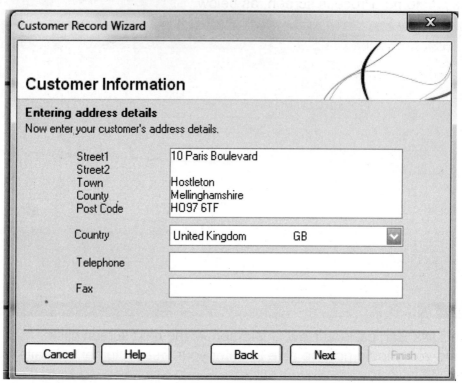

As with the supplier entry process, the next screen will ask you for further contact details, such as email and website addresses. You do not need to enter any information here at this point, so press the NEXT button.

Now you can enter the credit limit for this customer (this represents the maximum value of goods or services we are prepared to sell to them on credit). Here, for Mr Garros, it is £500.

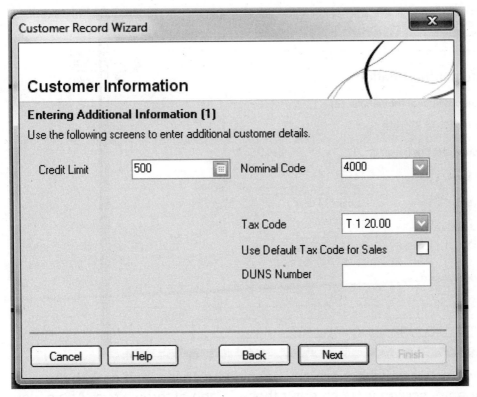

Leave the nominal code as 4000, and the tax code as T1 (20.00), as in the screen above. You will learn more about these shortly.

Now you can enter the credit terms. For Mr Garros we will require payment within fourteen days, and there is no settlement discount for early payment. Be careful to enter all information accurately and correctly at every stage of this process – check that the details you have entered match the source data.

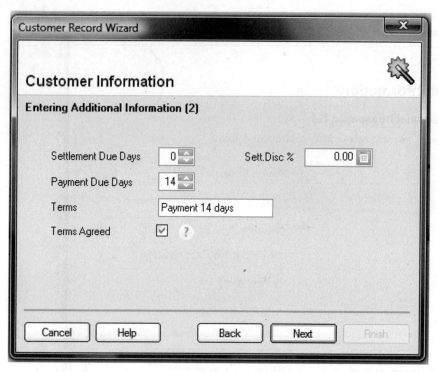

SAGE will now ask if there are any opening balances, and as with the supplier entry screen you can enter these in one of three ways. Again, you should choose to enter them as a single value.

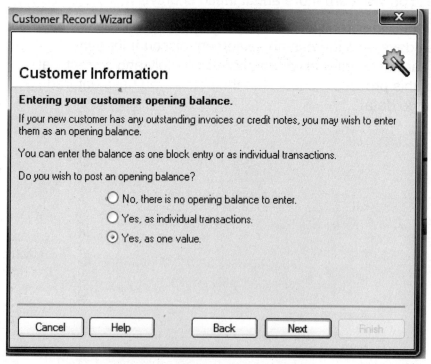

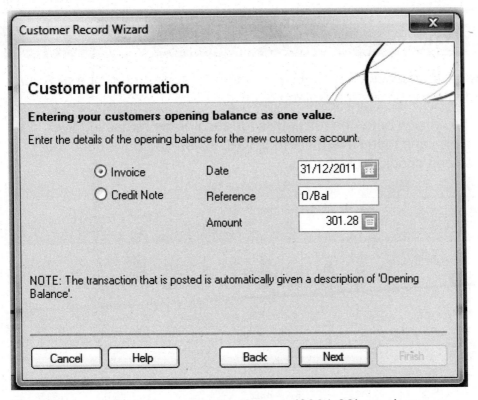

Enter the opening balance for Mr Garros (£301.28) as above.

SAGE now asks you to confirm the details you have entered and to save them. Again, this is an important stage of the process.

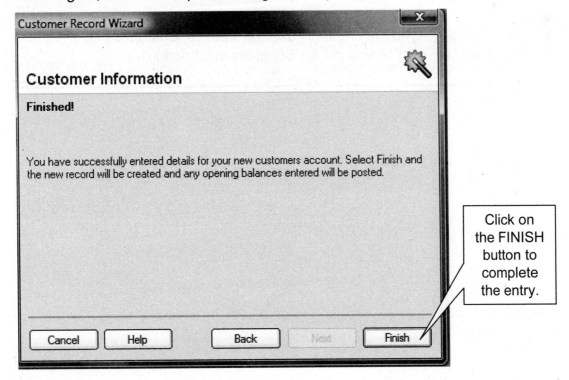

Click on the FINISH button to complete the entry.

Activity

Refer back to pages 55 and 56. You have already entered one of Wynn Bowlden's customers (Mr Roland Garros).

You should now enter the full details for each of the remaining five customers, and then save them to SAGE. When you have done this your screen should look like this:

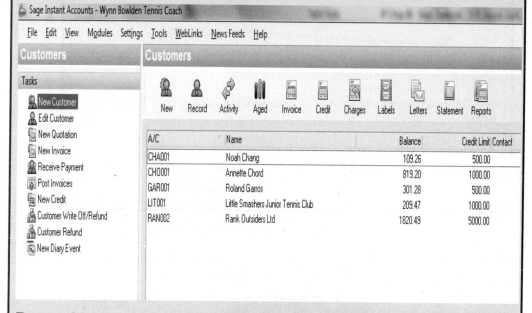

Remember – you may need to Change View to 'Customers' to see the list like this – just as you did for Suppliers in Chapter 5.

3 Printing customer data reports

You have entered the details of the six customers, so let's now check that they are correct by running off a report from SAGE.

The first report to print is the Customer List. The Report Browser for Customers works in the same way as for Suppliers – refer to Chapter 5 to remind yourself of this.

From the **Customers** window, click on **Reports** to open the Report Browser.

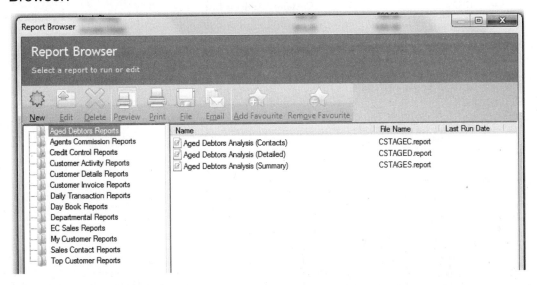

This will produce a new window with a list of customer-related reports that you could want to print and use. You will practice accessing some more of these later on, but for now the one that you want is the report entitled *Customer Address List*. This is contained within the folder called *Customer Details Reports* – to access the contents of this (or any) folder simply double-click on it.

Double click on *Customer Address List* to produce the report.

On the next screen you can identify the criteria by which you wish to select the contents of your report. As you wish to see a list of all the customers that you have entered keep the boxes as shown overleaf, then press OK.

You can use these boxes to filter which customers you want to appear in the report. Leave them as *'blank'* and *'ZZZZZZZ'* to show all customers

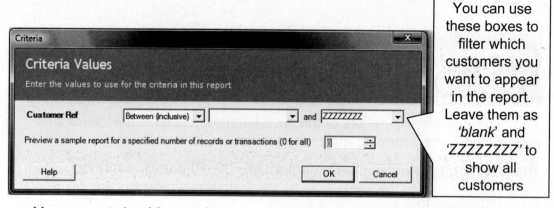

Your report should now show on screen, similar to the one below.

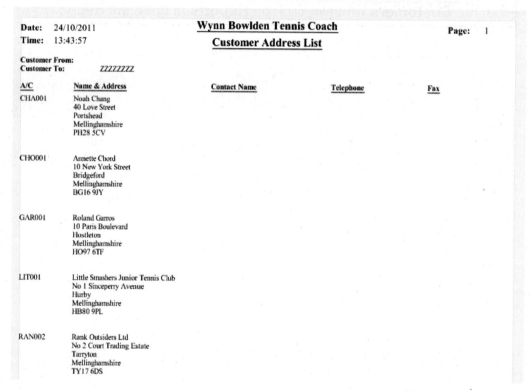

There are many other supplier reports available in this section – you should now feel confident enough to access these and to print them out. The exact list of reports that you will use will depend on your particular requirements, and you will see some of the more common ones later in this manual.

Product lines for sale

7

CONTENTS

1 Introduction

SAGE allows you to differentiate between sales of different types of products. This screen (within the Configuration Editor seen earlier) is used to set the defaults.

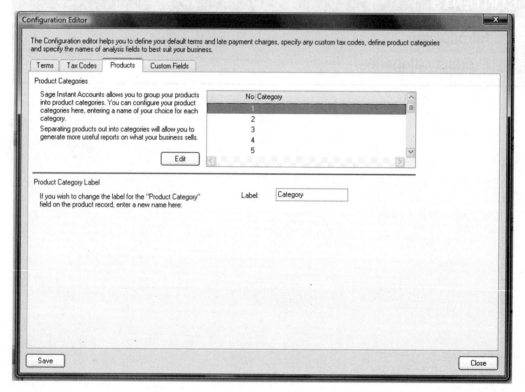

2 Product categories

You are going to set up five different product categories, as follows:

(1)   Tennis Racquets

(2)   Tennis Balls

(3)   Clothing – Men

(4)   Clothing – Women

(5)   Footwear

SAGE Instant v.17 will allow you to enter up to 999 different categories of product – but these five will suffice for now!

To amend a product category, use your cursor to highlight the number with a blue bar, and then click [Edit]. You can then easily type in your new description.

You should now set up the five product categories for Wynn Bowlden, as outlined above.

Your screen should now look like the one below.

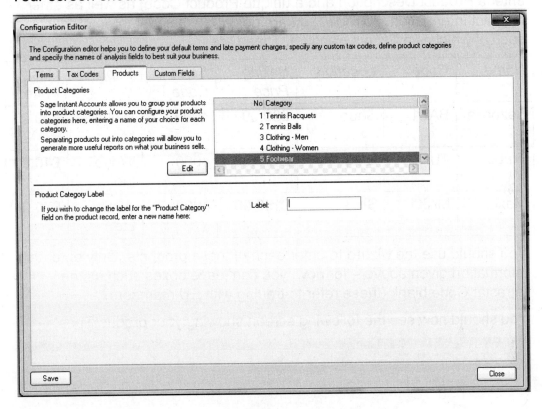

You should now click on the [Save] button and save the changes.

You can of course add new product categories at any time.

3   Product s

In order to set up different product lines, select **MODULES – PRODUCTS – NEW.** This launches the New Product Wizard, which requires you to enter a Product Description and a unique Product Code, as well as other relevant information. For now, you are going to enter just three products, each of which is a Tennis Racquet. These are:

Name	Code	Location	Selling Price	Sales Code	Supplier	Cost Price
Bazooka	BAZ1	Shop	£80.00	4000	Wotta Ltd	£30.00
Turbo	TUR1	Shop	£100.00	4000	Wotta Ltd	£40.00
Maxi	MAX1	Shop	£150.00	4000	Wotta Ltd	£70.00

You should use the wizard to enter each of these products. Only enter the information given above – for now, you can leave boxes such as the Intrastat Code blank (these refer to trading with EU members)

You should now see the following screen showing your product lines.

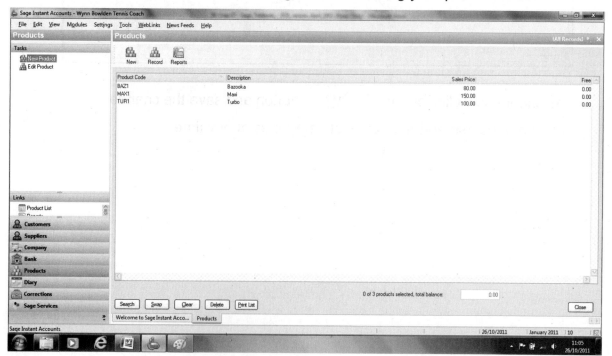

The nominal ledger

CONTENTS

1 Introduction
2 Entering a nominal code
3 Printing a trial balance

1 Introduction

The nominal ledger is probably the most important element of the SAGE (or indeed any) accounting system. This is simply a series of different accounts into which money is debited (paid in) or credited (taken out) each time a transaction is recorded.

Each of these accounts is given a unique four digit code number. To view the list of Nominal Codes go to the COMPANY screen, and then NOMINAL LEDGER.

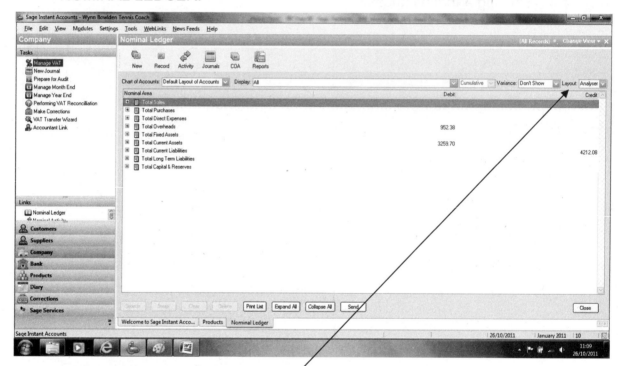

Select **'List'** from the layout menu.

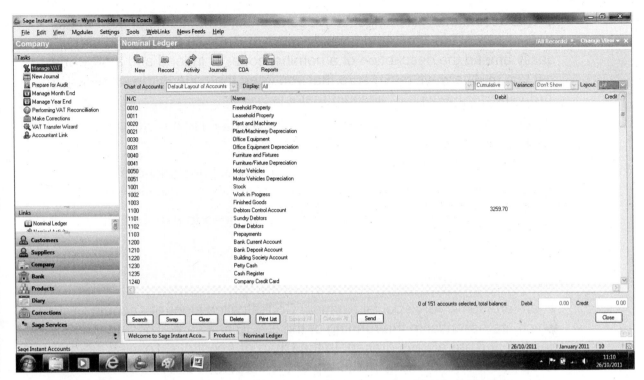

This now shows you a list of all of the nominal codes (N/Cs) for the business.

The four-digit code is important, as the list is actually broken down into groups:

0000-0999	Fixed Assets and Depreciation (e.g. Buildings, Equipment)
1000-1999	Current Assets (e.g. Stock, Debtors, Bank)
2000-2299	Short Term Liabilities (e.g. Creditors)
2300-2999	Long Term Liabilities (e.g. Loans)
3000-3999	Capital and Reserves
4000-4999	Sales
5000-5999	Purchases
6000-6999	Direct Expenses (e.g. Direct Labour)
7000-7999	Miscellaneous Overheads (e.g. Phone, Rent, Postage)
8000-8999	Bad debts and Depreciation
9000-9999	Suspense and Mispostings

SAGE uses these 'groupings' of codes to ensure that items appear in the correct part of the Profit and Loss Account or Balance Sheet. You can easily amend the description of a nominal code, or indeed add a new one, but you must always make sure that you keep the code in the correct 'grouping' for the type of account that it is.

You should now print out the list of nominal codes. Do this by simply pressing the Print List button.

The full list of default Nominal Codes should now print, taking approximately three pages.

You should now keep this list safe, as you will need to use it when entering transactions in the future.

Control Accounts

There are some very special Nominal Codes called Control Accounts, which are essential to the running of the SAGE software. These cannot be deleted and are always present in the Chart of Accounts. To view them go to SETTINGS (in the tabs at the top of the screen) – CONTROL ACCOUNTS. This will show you the main Control Accounts within SAGE, as shown below.

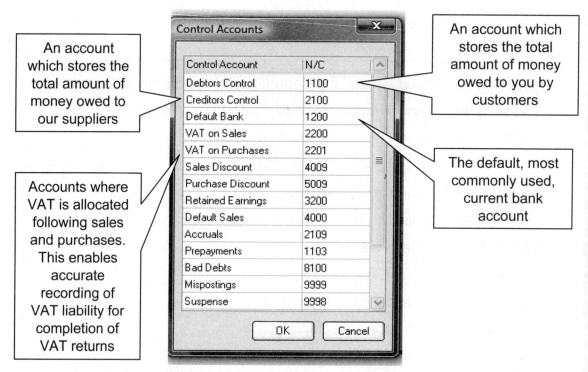

An account which stores the total amount of money owed to our suppliers

An account which stores the total amount of money owed to you by customers

Accounts where VAT is allocated following sales and purchases. This enables accurate recording of VAT liability for completion of VAT returns

The default, most commonly used, current bank account

Control Account	N/C
Debtors Control	1100
Creditors Control	2100
Default Bank	1200
VAT on Sales	2200
VAT on Purchases	2201
Sales Discount	4009
Purchase Discount	5009
Retained Earnings	3200
Default Sales	4000
Accruals	2109
Prepayments	1103
Bad Debts	8100
Mispostings	9999
Suspense	9998

Most of these accounts are used automatically by SAGE. This means that you do not need to specify them individually when entering transactions – SAGE will work out which control account is required and apply it automatically. Other Nominal Codes (from the list you printed out) will need to be entered.

2 Entering a nominal code

The default Chart of Accounts contains the most common codes set up for a general business. However, you will almost certainly want to add to, or amend, these Nominal Codes to suit your business in particular.

For example, Wynn Bowlden will want to be more specific when recording its sales and purchases. Have a look at your listing of Nominal Codes. Find the 5000-5999 Range (remember, these are set aside for Purchases).

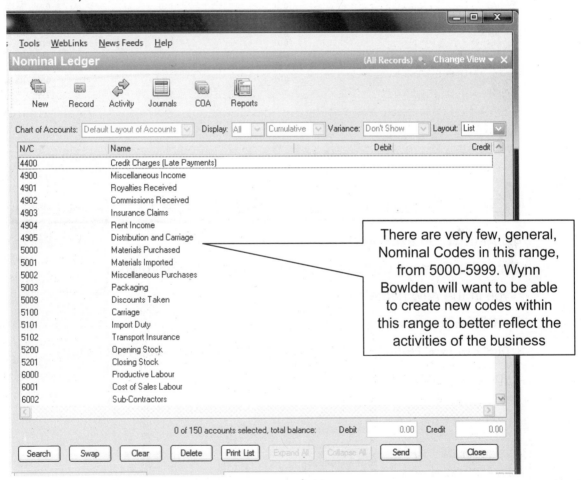

There are very few, general, Nominal Codes in this range, from 5000-5999. Wynn Bowlden will want to be able to create new codes within this range to better reflect the activities of the business

Now, from within the NOMINAL module click on the Record button.

You should now have a blank record screen, as below.

Month	Actuals	Budgets	To end Sep 2009
B/F	0.00	0.00	0.00
Oct	0.00	0.00	0.00
Nov	0.00	0.00	0.00
Dec	0.00	0.00	0.00
Jan	0.00	0.00	0.00
Feb	0.00	0.00	0.00
Mar	0.00	0.00	0.00
Apr	0.00	0.00	0.00
May	0.00	0.00	0.00
Jun	0.00	0.00	0.00
Jul	0.00	0.00	0.00
Aug	0.00	0.00	0.00
Sep	0.00	0.00	0.00
Future	0.00	0.00	0.00
Total	0.00	0.00	0.00

To **AMEND** an existing code:

Enter the Nominal Code (or select from the pull down menu)

Type in the new name

To **CREATE** a new code:

Enter the new Nominal Code (making sure it is in the correct range)

Type in the new name

Exercise

To practice amending and creating Nominal Codes, enter each of the following N/Cs and names. Do them one by one, and then save each one.

SALES		PURCHASES	
Nominal Code	*Name*	*Nominal Code*	*Name*
4000	Sales –Equipment	5000	Purchases – Equipment
4001	Sales – Clothing and Footwear	5001	Purchases – Clothing and Footwear
4002	Sales – Individual Coaching	5002	Purchases – Stationery
4003	Sales – Group Coaching	5003	Purchases – Packaging
4004	Sales – Other	5004	Purchases – Other Consumables

Once you have entered these, close down the window and generate the Nominal List report for the range 4000-5999. You do this by using the Report Browser as before, but this time within the Financials section of SAGE. You will find the Nominal List Report in the folder named **Nominal Details Reports**.

To select the range 4000-5999 use the Range Selection Screen:

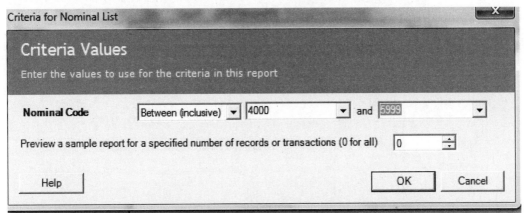

The report should look like this:

Date: 26/10/2011	**Wynn Bowlden Tennis Coach**
Time: 11:25:33	**Nominal List**

N/C From:	4000
N/C To:	5999

N/C	Name
4000	Sales - Equipment
4001	Sales - Clothing and Footwear
4002	Sales - Individual Coaching
4003	Sales - Group Coaching
4004	Sales - Other
4009	Discounts Allowed
4099	Flat Rate - Benefit/Cost
4100	Sales Type D
4101	Sales Type E
4200	Sales of Assets
4400	Credit Charges (Late Payments)
4900	Miscellaneous Income
4901	Royalties Received
4902	Commissions Received
4903	Insurance Claims
4904	Rent Income
4905	Distribution and Carriage
5000	Purchases - Equipment
5001	Purchases - Clothing and Footwear
5002	Purchases - Stationery
5003	Purchases - Packaging
5004	Purchases - Other Consumables
5009	Discounts Taken
5100	Carriage
5101	Import Duty
5102	Transport Insurance
5200	Opening Stock
5201	Closing Stock

Note the new sales categories here ← (pointing to 4002 Sales - Individual Coaching)

Note the new purchases categories here ← (pointing to 5003 Purchases - Packaging)

KAPLAN PUBLISHING

Well done! Now you can amend or create new nominal codes. The next step is to post opening balances to each relevant nominal code within SAGE for your business. This means that you will be entering the financial balance on each account for Wynn Bowlden, as at the first date you begin using the SAGE system to record financial transactions for the company. Remember for Wynn Bowlden this was 31st December 2011. The list of opening balances is shown below:

Wynn Bowlden

Opening Balances

	Nominal code	Debit	Credit	
Motor vehicles (at cost)	0050	8000.00		
Depreciation (Motor Vehicles)	0051		2000.00	
Office Equipment	0030	3420.00		
Depreciation (Office Equipment)	0031		1710.00	
Stock (as at 1st January 2011)	1001	2865.90		
Debtors Control Account	1100	3259.70		*Note:* This is the total of the suppliers' balances that you entered earlier. This has already been entered and so will not need to be entered again.
Petty Cash	1230	100.00		
Bank	1200	12416.60		
Creditors Control Account	2100		4212.08	
VAT Liability	2202		981.61	
Capital	3000		3500.00	Similarly this is the total of the individual customers' accounts that you entered earlier. Again, this will not need to be entered again.
Profit and Loss Account	3200		4121.14	
Sales – Equipment	4000		2016.53	
Sales – Clothing and Footwear	4001		2195.46	
Sales – Individual Coaching	4002		13229.30	
Sales – Group Coaching	4003		13450.50	
Sales – Other	4004		601.60	
Purchases – Equipment	5000	1015.20		
Purchases – Clothing and Footwear	5001	1310.60		
Purchases – Stationery	5002	415.20		
Purchases – Packaging	5003	208.78		
Purchases – Other Consumables	5004	104.61		
Rent	7100	3600.00		
General Rates	7103	350.00		
Telephone	7502	491.52		
Miscellaneous Motor Expenses	7304	8604.47		
General expenses	8207	1855.64		
		48018.22	**48018.22**	

Entering a new balance

Entering opening balances in SAGE is very straightforward.

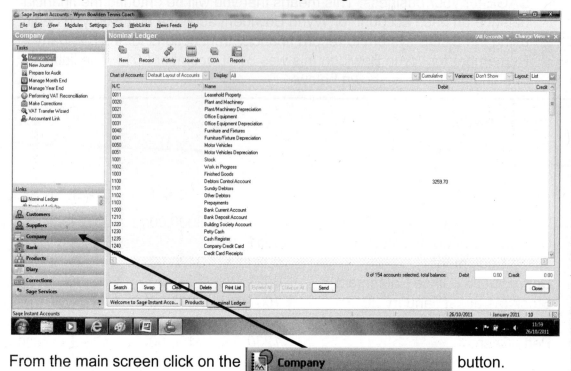

From the main screen click on the **Company** button.

Highlight the Nominal Code for which you want to enter an opening balance.

The first amount we need to enter is for Motor Vehicles – the amount is £8,000. This is a **debit balance**, because it represents the cost of the motor vehicles (a fixed asset) owned by the business. You can see that Motor Vehicles has been automatically assigned a Nominal Code of **0050** by SAGE.

Double-click your mouse on this code.

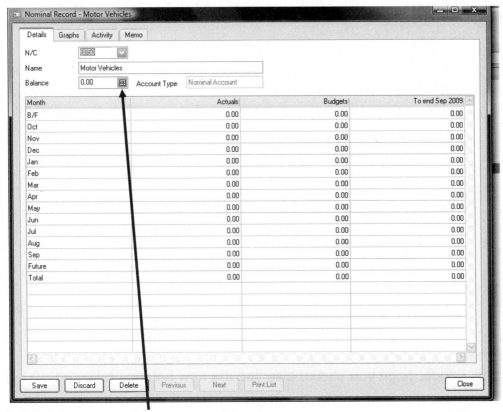

Now click on the 'Opening Balance' icon.

Keep the Ref as "O/Bal". Change the date box to 31st December 2011 if necessary and enter the opening balance amount of £8,000.00 in the Debit box. Leave the credit box at zero. Then click the Save button.

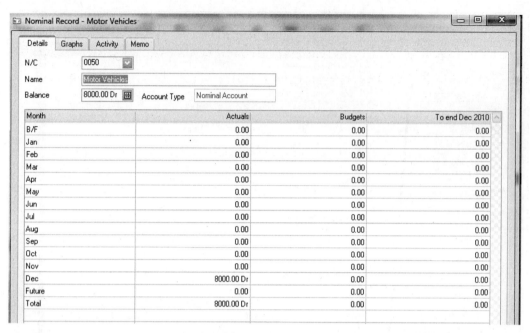

Notice how the detail record for Nominal Code 0050 (Motor Vehicles) has now changed, showing your entry in December. When you return to the Nominal Ledger page you should also see the new balance reflected there.

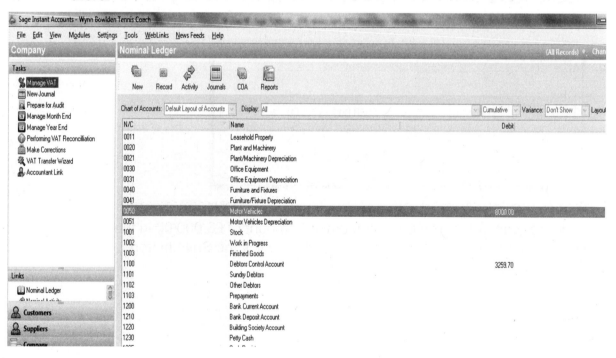

Exercise

You should now be able to enter the opening balances for each of the accounts.

Important

1   You will need to create a new Nominal Codes for the balance for General Expenses (use code 8207), and amend the name of the account for code 3000 to "Capital"

2   You do not need to enter opening balances for two items, the Debtors Control Account and the Creditors Control Account. This is because these represent the total amount owed to us (debtors) and the total amount we owe (creditors), made up of all of the individual balances you entered earlier. These control account balances are therefore calculated automatically by SAGE and you do not enter them.

3   Be careful to enter each balance correctly as either a **debit** or a **credit** balance.

3 Printing a trial balance

You have now entered all the opening balances for Wynn Bowlden. You are now ready to begin entering transactions on a day to day basis. Before that though, you should print off a Trial Balance.

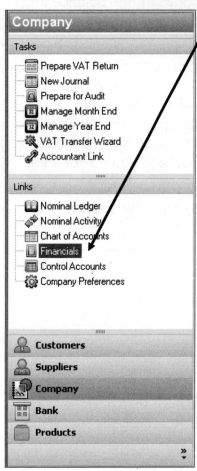

From the Company screen, select "Financials" in the links section.

This will create a new screen, from which you can quickly produce a series of the most useful reports in SAGE, including the Trial Balance, the Balance Sheet and the Profit and Loss Account. Double-click on 'Financials' to show this screen.

From the toolbar at the top of the Financials screen:

Select the  Trial icon.

You are now asked to select how you want to view the report.

For now, you will just preview the report (i.e. view it on screen). Select this and then press the ⬚Run⬚ button.

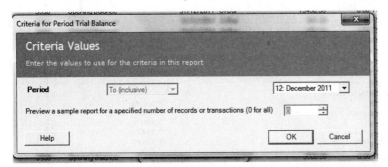

You want to view the trial balance as at December 2011, to see all of the opening balances you have entered. Make sure you amend the date box to show December 2011. Leave the next box as 0, and click OK

This should bring up a trial balance showing balances as at 31st December 2011. You may need to maximize the screen to see the whole report on screen – do this by clicking the *maximize* icon in the top right corner of the window ( )

If you have entered everything correctly you should see that both columns (debit and credit) balance to **£48,108.22**.

You should now print out this trial balance and keep it safe.

Hopefully you have entered all the balances correctly and your Trial Balance is therefore correct. In the Trial Balance overleaf, however, it is apparent that there has been a mistake made in the data entry. SAGE has balanced the debits and credits by introducing a **SUSPENSE ACCOUNT** (Code 9998). On further inspection it can be seen that the figure for General Expenses (Code 8207) has been entered as £2855.64 instead of £1855.64. This must now be corrected.

There are a number of ways to make corrections in SAGE – one of the most common is via a **JOURNAL**. The journal can be found in **COMPANY – FINANCIALS.** Here a correcting journal has been produced, crediting General Expenses (Code 8207) with £1000 and debiting Suspense Account (9998) with the same amount.

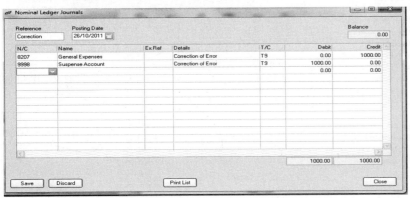

Date:	26/10/2011	**Wynn Bowlden Tennis Coach**		Page:	1
Time:	12:21:08	**Period Trial Balance**			

To Period: Month 12, December 2011

N/C	Name	Debit	Credit
0030	Office Equipment	3,420.00	
0031	Office Equipment Depreciation		1,710.00
0050	Motor Vehicles	8,000.00	
0051	Motor Vehicles Depreciation		2,000.00
1001	Stock	2,865.90	
1100	Debtors Control Account	3,259.70	
1200	Bank Current Account	12,416.60	
1230	Petty Cash	100.00	
2100	Creditors Control Account		4,212.08
2202	VAT Liability		981.61
3000	Capital		3,500.00
3200	Profit and Loss Account		4,121.14
4000	Sales - Equipment		2,016.53
4001	Sales - Clothing and Footwear		2,195.46
4002	Sales - Individual Coaching		13,229.30
4003	Sales - Group Coaching		13,450.50
4004	Sales - Other		601.60
5000	Purchases - Equipment	1,015.20	
5001	Purchases - Clothing and Footwear	1,310.60	
5002	Purchases - Stationery	415.20	
5003	Purchases - Packaging	208.78	
5004	Purchases - Other Consumables	104.61	
7100	Rent	3,600.00	
7103	General Rates	350.00	
7304	Miscellaneous Motor Expenses	8,604.47	
7502	Telephone	491.52	
8207	General Expenses	2,855.64	
9998	Suspense Account		1,000.00
	Totals:	49,018.22	49,018.22

> Notice the suspense account indicating an error

Date:	26/10/2011	**Wynn Bowlden Tennis Coach**		Page:	1
Time:	12:41:43	**Period Trial Balance**			

To Period: Month 12, December 2011

N/C	Name	Debit	Credit
0030	Office Equipment	3,420.00	
0031	Office Equipment Depreciation		1,710.00
0050	Motor Vehicles	8,000.00	
0051	Motor Vehicles Depreciation		2,000.00
1001	Stock	2,865.90	
1100	Debtors Control Account	3,259.70	
1200	Bank Current Account	12,416.60	
1230	Petty Cash	100.00	
2100	Creditors Control Account		4,212.08
2202	VAT Liability		981.61
3000	Capital		3,500.00
3200	Profit and Loss Account		4,121.14
4000	Sales - Equipment		2,016.53
4001	Sales - Clothing and Footwear		2,195.46
4002	Sales - Individual Coaching		13,229.30
4003	Sales - Group Coaching		13,450.50
4004	Sales - Other		601.60
5000	Purchases - Equipment	1,015.20	
5001	Purchases - Clothing and Footwear	1,310.60	
5002	Purchases - Stationery	415.20	
5003	Purchases - Packaging	208.78	
5004	Purchases - Other Consumables	104.61	
7100	Rent	3,600.00	
7103	General Rates	350.00	
7304	Miscellaneous Motor Expenses	8,604.47	
7502	Telephone	491.52	
8207	General Expenses	1,855.64	
	Totals:	48,018.22	48,018.22

> The journal has corrected the error and there is no suspense account

Entering transactions

9

CONTENTS

1   Introduction

Any business will carry out a wide range of transactions every day of the week. However, the majority of these will fall into one of the following categories:

Credit transactions

- Purchases of stock on credit

- Sales of goods or services on credit

Cash transactions

- Purchases made by cash/cheque/card

- Sales made for cash/cheque/card

- Payments made to suppliers (for goods/services bought on credit)

- Receipts from customers (for goods/services sold on credit)

- Payments made to meet other expenses

- Payment of salaries and wages to staff

- Petty cash transactions

- Transactions directly through the bank account (e.g. bank charges, interest, direct debits, standing orders)

Each of these transactions will have an effect on two accounts within the SAGE system – this is the underlying principle of double-entry bookkeeping. However, SAGE simplifies this by carrying out much of the double entry automatically.

Firstly, consider the first type of transactions – purchases and sales made on credit. This means that a legally binding contract is established between the two parties, and (usually) the goods or services are supplied but payment is not paid until some later date. The key document in this process is the invoice – as this is the document which demands payment and lays down the agreed terms of the transaction.

Hence entering a credit transaction (whether a purchase or a sale) is a two stage process in SAGE:

1   Enter the details of the invoice against the relevant supplier or customer. This will establish the presence and value of the legally binding debt.

2   At a later date, enter the details of the payment of the debt.

Note that this approach is applicable for both credit sales and credit purchases – you just have to be sure to enter the details in the correct part of SAGE.

Now consider the second type of transactions – each of these has a direct impact on one or other of the bank accounts within SAGE. Note that SAGE classes accounts such as cash in hand and petty cash as 'bank accounts' – they are all current assets within the Balance Sheet.

2 Credit sales – batching customer invoices

Wynn Bowlden has a number of credit customers on 31st December 2011. Each of these has been issued with an invoice, but these invoices now need to be entered into SAGE.

The easiest way to do this is to *batch* invoices together so that they can be input at the same time.

To enter a batch of customer (sales) invoices go to the **CUSTOMERS** module and then press the **BATCH INVOICE** button [Batch Invoice] on the Links Panel.

You will now need to insert data into the next screen as follows:

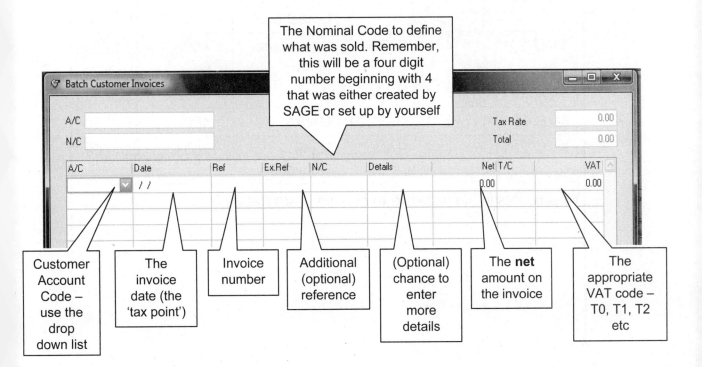

The Nominal Code to define what was sold. Remember, this will be a four digit number beginning with 4 that was either created by SAGE or set up by yourself

Customer Account Code – use the drop down list

The invoice date (the 'tax point')

Invoice number

Additional (optional) reference

(Optional) chance to enter more details

The **net** amount on the invoice

The appropriate VAT code – T0, T1, T2 etc

Some Important Keys / Shortcuts

F6 (found at the top of your keyboard) – *this will duplicate the field above.*

[Calc. Net] This is a really useful shortcut which can be used where you know the **gross amount** of an invoice (i.e. including VAT) but do not have the **net amount**. Simply enter the gross amount in the net box and then press the [Calc. Net] button – this will calculate the net amount and the VAT for you.

Once you have entered all invoices in the batch you should then review them to ensure you have entered them correctly, and then [Save] them.

This will post the invoices to SAGE and update the system accordingly.

Exercise

Enter the following six invoices for Wynn Bowlden using the batch invoicing method. Note that you will also have to create a new customer account for G Bates – you learned how to do this in Chapter 6.

Date	Invoice No	A/c No	Customer	Nominal Code	Net Amount
31/12/2011	1	CHA001	Chang	4001	£58.33
31/12/2011	2	CHO001	Chord	4002	£60.00
31/12/2011	3	LIT001	Little Smashers	4003	£220.00
31/12/2011	4	BAT001	Bates *(see below)*	4002	£120.00
31/12/2011	5	CHO001	Chord	4002	£30.00
31/12/2011	6	GAR001	Garros	4002	£60.00
31/12/2011	7	RAN002	Rank Outsiders	4003	£240.00

All amounts in the table are **exclusive** of VAT at 20.0%

New Customer Details

Mr G Bates
12 Main Street
Miltonby
Mellinghamshire
MN87 4DF

A/c Ref BAT001

Credit terms: Payment in 14 days

Credit Limit: £1000.00

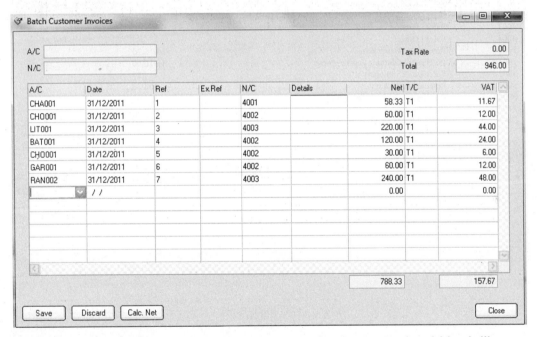

When you have entered all seven invoices, your screen should look like this. Check for accuracy, and when you are happy press the

[Save] button.

Now print out another Trial Balance for December 2011. Compare the two reports and identify the changes that have occurred.

Here is a copy of the Trial Balance produced earlier.

Date:	26/10/2011	**Wynn Bowlden Tennis Coach**	Page: 1
Time:	12:41:43	**Period Trial Balance**	

To Period: Month 12, December 2011

N/C	Name	Debit	Credit
0030	Office Equipment	3,420.00	
0031	Office Equipment Depreciation		1,710.00
0050	Motor Vehicles	8,000.00	
0051	Motor Vehicles Depreciation		2,000.00
1001	Stock	2,865.90	
1100	Debtors Control Account	3,259.70	
1200	Bank Current Account	12,416.60	
1230	Petty Cash	100.00	
2100	Creditors Control Account		4,212.08
2202	VAT Liability		981.61
3000	Capital		3,500.00
3200	Profit and Loss Account		4,121.14
4000	Sales - Equipment		2,016.53
4001	Sales - Clothing and Footwear		2,195.46
4002	Sales - Individual Coaching		13,229.30
4003	Sales - Group Coaching		13,450.50
4004	Sales - Other		601.60
5000	Purchases - Equipment	1,015.20	
5001	Purchases - Clothing and Footwear	1,310.60	
5002	Purchases - Stationery	415.20	
5003	Purchases - Packaging	208.78	
5004	Purchases - Other Consumables	104.61	
7100	Rent	3,600.00	
7103	General Rates	350.00	
7304	Miscellaneous Motor Expenses	8,604.47	
7502	Telephone	491.52	
8207	General Expenses	1,855.64	
	Totals:	48,018.22	48,018.22

Date:	26/10/2011	Wynn Bowlden Tennis Coach		Page:	1
Time:	13:55:25	Period Trial Balance			

To Period: Month 12, December 2011

N/C	Name	Debit	Credit	
0030	Office Equipment	3,420.00		
0031	Office Equipment Depreciation		1,710.00	
0050	Motor Vehicles	8,000.00		
0051	Motor Vehicles Depreciation		2,000.00	
1001	Stock	2,865.90		
1100	Debtors Control Account	4,205.70		❶
1200	Bank Current Account	12,416.60		
1230	Petty Cash	100.00		
2100	Creditors Control Account		4,212.08	
2200	Sales Tax Control Account		157.67	❷
2202	VAT Liability		981.61	
3000	Capital		3,500.00	
3200	Profit and Loss Account		4,121.14	
4000	Sales - Equipment		2,016.53	
4001	Sales - Clothing and Footwear		2,253.79	❸
4002	Sales - Individual Coaching		13,499.30	
4003	Sales - Group Coaching		13,910.50	
4004	Sales - Other		601.60	
5000	Purchases - Equipment	1,015.20		
5001	Purchases - Clothing and Footwear	1,310.60		
5002	Purchases - Stationery	415.20		
5003	Purchases - Packaging	208.78		
5004	Purchases - Other Consumables	104.61		
7100	Rent	3,600.00		
7103	General Rates	350.00		
7304	Miscellaneous Motor Expenses	8,604.47		
7502	Telephone	491.52		
8207	General Expenses	1,855.64		
	Totals:	**48,964.22**	**48,964.22**	

Notice which figures have changed.

(1)   N/C 1100 (Debtors control account) has increased to £4205.70. This reflects the fact that Wynn Bowlden is now owed an additional £946.00 by its debtors.

(2)   N/Cs 4001, 4002 and 4003 have increased, representing the new sales that the company made on 31st December. Note that the increase in these figures is the **net** increase in sales.

(3)   There is a new Nominal Code (2200) called 'Sales Tax Control Account'. This control account automatically records all output VAT (on sales). There is a similar control account for input VAT (on purchases). The two control accounts are used to calculate and produce the company's VAT Return. The amount on this code is currently £157.67 (a **credit** balance) – the VAT charged on all the sales invoices you have entered.

The increase in **debit** entries (£1055.75) equals the increase in **credit** entries (£898.50 plus £157.25) – the principles of double entry bookkeeping have been met and SAGE has actually done the double entries for you.

3 Posting credit notes

A credit note is essentially a 'negative invoice' and is produced and sent to customers when a refund of money is needed. The most likely time this will happen is when goods that the organization has sold to a customer have been returned as faulty. They can also be used to correct errors etc.

Producing a credit note in SAGE is straightforward and effectively mirrors the process for producing an invoice.

Let us suppose that the coaching session booked by Annette Chord (Invoice Number 5), for which she paid £30.00 plus VAT, is cancelled and Wynn Bowlden agrees to issue a credit note to the customer.

From the **CUSTOMER** module select **CUSTOMER LIST** and then from the icons at the top of the screen select the [Credit] icon.

Here you can enter a batch of Credit Notes (just as you did with the batched invoices). SAGE shows your entries in RED to make it obvious that this is a Credit Note.

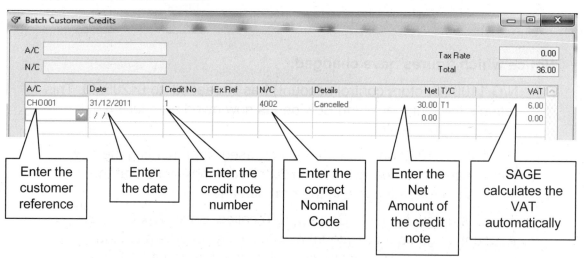

When you have entered all Credit Notes in the batch, and checked their accuracy, **SAVE** them to ensure that SAGE can process them.

4 Producing customer statements

Having produced and sent invoices to customers, most businesses will also need to send periodic (usually monthly) statements to their customers which will list all new transactions – such as new purchases, payments received, credit notes issued etc.

SAGE allows the easy creation and production of customer statements.

Firstly, from the **CUSTOMER** module (in **LIST** display), press the Statement button.

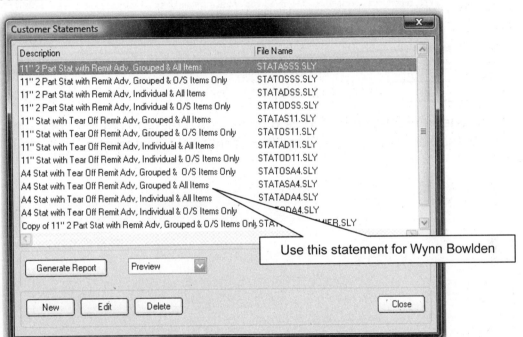

This provides a choice of different statement layouts. You should use the one which best suits your business needs; however, for the purposes of this manual you should use the one called 'A4 Stat with Tear off Remit. Adv. Grouped & All Items'. Select this one by double-clicking.

In the **CRITERIA** screen (see overleaf) use the pull-down menus to select customer Chord (Ref CHO001). You can use the 'From...to...' feature to select a range of customers – but for now just select the one.

Make sure the Transaction dates are '01/12/2011' to '31/12/2011' – this will ensure that all transactions in September are shown.

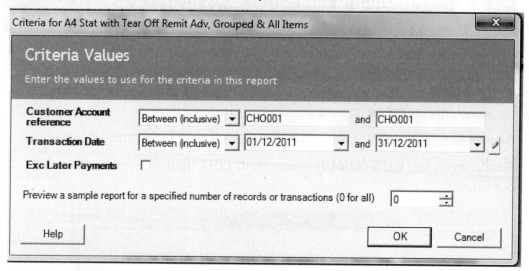

Press [OK] to create the report.

This statement (shown on the next page) could then be printed out (using special stationery if required) and then sent to the customer.

Wynn Bowldon Tennis Coach
15 Love Street
Pickerton
Mellinghamshire
ML40 3TT

Wynn Bowldon Tennis Coach
15 Love Street
Pickerton
Mellinghamshire
ML40 3TT

	CHO001
Annette Chord	
10 New York Street	31/12/2011
Bridgeford	
Mellinghamshire	
BG16 9JY	1

	CHO001
Annette Chord	
10 New York Street	31/12/2011
Bridgeford	
Mellinghamshire	
BG16 9JY	1

NOTE: **All values are shown in Pound Sterling**

NOTE: All values are shown in   **Pound Sterling**

31/12/11	O/Bal	Goods/Services	819.20 ♦	
31/12/11	2	Goods/Services	72.00 ♦	
31/12/11	5	Goods/Services	36.00 ♦	
31/12/11	1	Credit	♦	36.00

31/12/11	Goods/Services	819.20	
31/12/11	Goods/Services	72.00	
31/12/11	Goods/Services	36.00	
31/12/11	Credit		36.00

£   891.20   £   0.00   £   0.00   £   0.00   £   0.00

£   891.20

£   891.20

5 Credit purchases

When an organization purchases goods or services on credit, it will receive an invoice from the supplier. These must be recorded immediately in SAGE, even though they may not be paid for some time.

The most common way to process supplier invoices is to *batch* them (in much the same way as you did with the invoices to customers). This way, a number of invoices can be processed at the same time.

The process for entering batches of supplier invoices is very similar to that for entering batches of customer invoices – except it is accessed via the **SUPPLIERS** module.

You should enter the **SUPPLIERS** module now.

Press the icon in the Links Panel.

Wynn Bowlden received the following five invoices on 31st December 2011.

Invoice Ref	Invoice Date	Supplier	Account	Net amount	Nominal Code
1892	29/12/11	Kike Shoes	KS001	£308.30	5001
309	29/12/11	First Serve Office Supplies	FS001	£220.00	5002
312	29/12/11	First Serve Office Supplies	FS001	£16.58	5002
2018	30/12/11	Wotta Rackets Ltd	WR001	£190.00	5000
40293	30/12/11	Wilkinson Tennis Balls	WT001	£49.50	5000

You should now enter the above five supplier invoices as a batch. You should use the **Invoice Date** shown above, rather than the date the invoice is actually received.

When you have done this the screen should look like this:

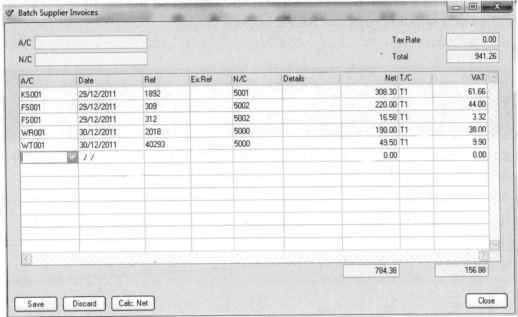

You should verify the entries and then press the **SAVE** button to post your entries to SAGE.

6 Supplier credit notes

These are processed in exactly the same way as you processed credit notes issued to customers.

Access the entry screen from the SUPPLIERS module, using the button.

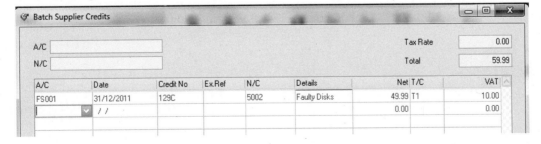

Wynn Bowlden receives one credit note. It is from First Serve Office Supplies on 31 December and is a credit for £49.99 (excluding VAT) for some discs that were returned as faulty. The credit note reference is 129C. The Nominal Code for this is 5002 (Purchases – Stationery).

You should enter this as follows:

Again – note that SAGE shows your entries in red so that they are easily identifiable as a credit note. When you have checked the accuracy of your entries you should press the **SAVE** button.

7 Bank transactions

SAGE allows you to run a number of 'bank accounts'. These need not necessarily all be held at a bank – they could also include cash in hand, petty cash etc.

The principles for making payments into or out of any of these accounts are the same.

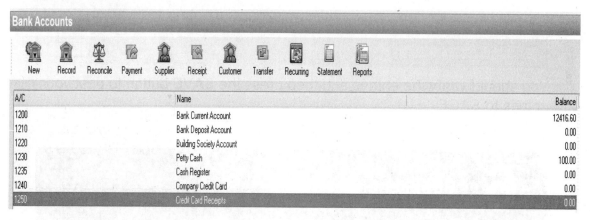

Enter the **Bank** module. You can see that SAGE has already set up a number of different bank accounts, each with its own Nominal Code. You can of course amend these or add to them if you wish.

The most commonly used bank account is probably Nominal Code 1200. This is the one that you will use in this manual for payments into and out of Wynn Bowlden's main current bank account. You can see that it has a balance at the moment of £12416.60. You may recall that this was the opening balance that you entered earlier. None of the entries that you have made since then have affected the bank balance.

8 Making payments

Wynn Bowlden has three payments to make on 31st December 2011. These are:

- A cheque for £102.35 (plus VAT at 20%) to Arrow Telecoms to pay the telephone bill – Cheque number 249

- A cheque for £35.00 to Pickerton Darts Association for advertising in their League Handbook (no VAT on this transaction) – Cheque number 250

- A cheque for £50.00 to Pickerton Borough Council for a parking permit (no VAT) – Cheque number 251

To enter these transactions, go to the **BANK** module, select the required bank account (in this case the current account) and click the

Payment

button, or select **NEW PAYMENT** from the Tasks Panel.

Enter each transaction as a separate line. Be careful to make sure you select the appropriate Nominal Code for the expense item, and also the correct VAT rate. If there is no VAT you should use Tax Code **T0**.

Your entries should look like this:

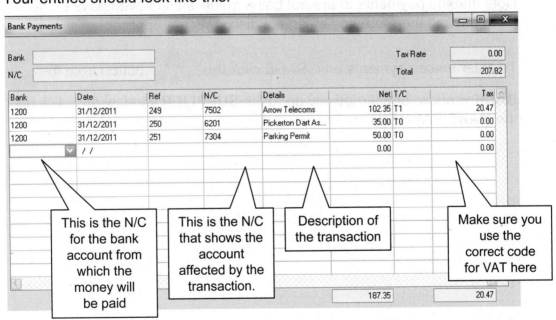

Bank	Date	Ref	N/C	Details	Net	T/C	Tax
1200	31/12/2011	249	7502	Arrow Telecoms	102.35	T1	20.47
1200	31/12/2011	250	6201	Pickerton Dart As...	35.00	T0	0.00
1200	31/12/2011	251	7304	Parking Permit	50.00	T0	0.00
	/ /				0.00		0.00

This is the N/C for the bank account from which the money will be paid

This is the N/C that shows the account affected by the transaction.

Description of the transaction

Make sure you use the correct code for VAT here

When you have checked your entries, **SAVE** them to SAGE.

Now check the balance on Nominal Code 1200 (the bank current account).

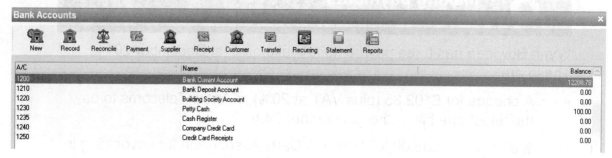

See how the bank balance has now gone down to £12208.78 – reflecting the fact that payments of £207.82 (£187.35 plus £20.47 VAT) have been taken from it.

Paying suppliers

Wynn Bowlden also decides to pay two outstanding creditors on 31st December, as follows:

First Serve Office Supplies (FS001)
Amount: £401.35 inc VAT   *Paid by cheque number 252*

Yonnad Tenniswear (YT001)
Amount £864.10 (inc VAT).   *Paid by cheque number 253*

Note that the payments to are not being made within seven days of the invoices, and therefore no settlement discounts are applicable.

To enter these payments onto SAGE click the button from the

BANK window, or alternatively go to the **SUPPLIER** window and click on the **MAKE PAYMENT** task.

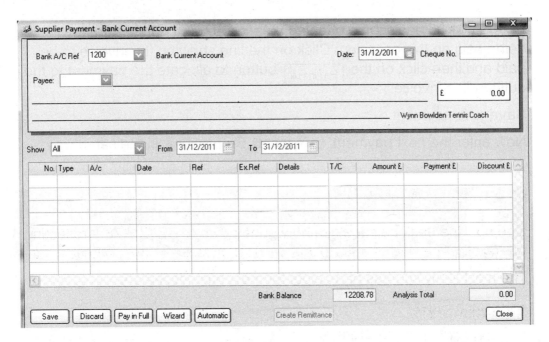

Use the drop down menu to select the first supplier to pay – in this case First Serve Office Supplies. Enter the correct date, the cheque number and the amount being paid (£401.35).

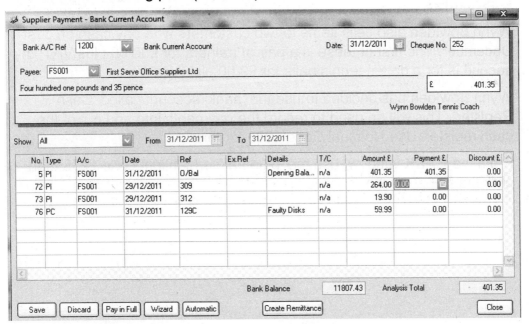

Note how SAGE has completed the bottom half of the screen with the outstanding invoices for this supplier. This allows you to decide which outstanding invoices you want to pay.

Enter £401.35 against the opening balance amount – this is the invoice being paid on this occasion. Click on the line showing the invoice to be paid and then click on the [Pay in Full] button to allocate the payment to the outstanding invoice.

Save your payment.

Now enter the next payment, to Yonnad Tenniswear, in the same way.

9 Recording receipts

The most likely sources of receipts for most businesses are:

- Cash Sales

- Receipts from Debtors

You will look at these in turn.

Cash sales

Wynn Bowlden also sells items to two customers who pay cash on 31st December. The first of these is a pair of trainers for £30.00 plus VAT; the second is for a dozen tennis balls for £9.00 plus VAT.

Wynn Bowlden has decided to use the 'bank' account called 'Cash Register'. This will be used to record the payments into and out of the cash register. Use Nominal Code 1235 for this.

From the **BANK** window, use the 'blue bar' to highlight code 1235 then click the   icon.

Receipt

Enter the two cash sales as below:

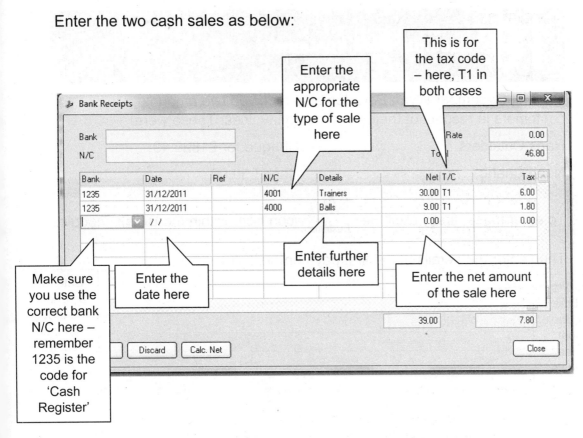

When you have entered both transactions press **SAVE**.

You should now see that there is a balance on N/C 1235 of £46.80 – the total amount of the two cash sales.

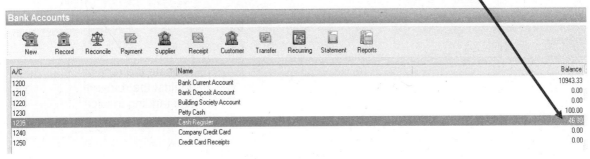

10 Receipts from customers

On 31st December Wynn Bowlden also received two amounts from customers in respect of their outstanding invoices. These were:

Rank Outsiders   Cheque for £1820.49

Noah Chang   Cash £50.00

To enter these, firstly click the icon from within the **BANK** module.

Then enter the details of the first payment as follows.

Be sure to select the correct Bank Account from the drop down list

Enter the amount of the cheque received

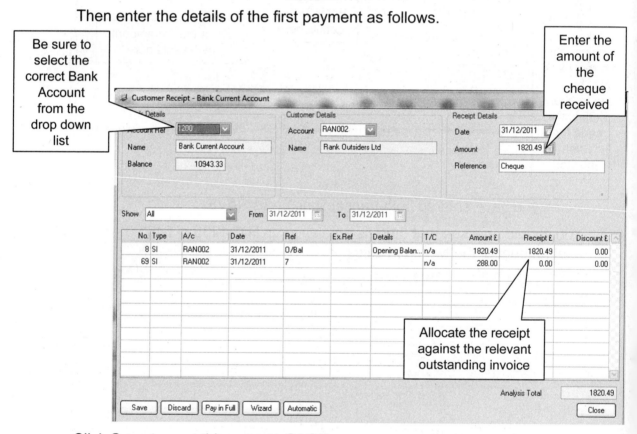

Allocate the receipt against the relevant outstanding invoice

Click **Save** to post this entry to SAGE.

Now enter the second receipt, from Noah Chang. Note that only £50.00 has been received, and that he paid in cash.

Your screen should look like this (note that the bank account has changed from 1200 to 1235):

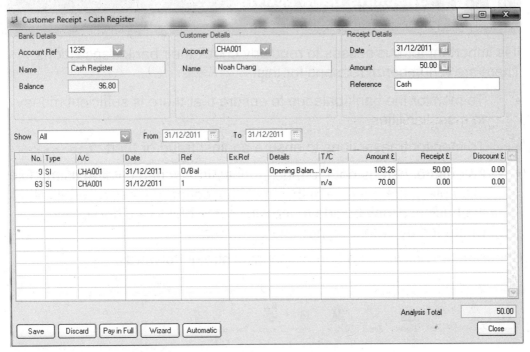

Again, click on **Save.**

When recording BACS receipts the same process should be followed however the date that the amount is received in the bank should be recorded as the date and the reference should generally be the name of the supplier so it ties in what appears with what appears on the bank receipt. This makes it easier to perform the bank reconciliation (see later on in the manual).

11 Checking bank activity

It is important for businesses to regularly check their bank transactions. There are a number of reasons for this:

- To monitor the bank balance to ensure that there is sufficient money to meet liabilities

- To monitor transactions to ensure against fraud or theft

- To ensure there is not too much money in any particular account. For example, if the balance in the current account reaches a certain level the business may decide to transfer some of it to a different account where it may earn a higher rate of interest.

Checking the activity on a bank account is straightforward.

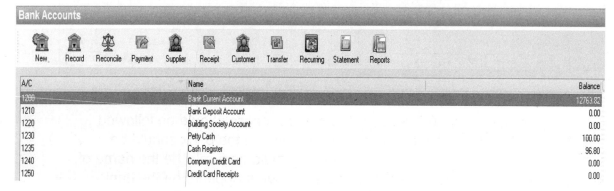

Highlight the account you want to check, and then double-click on it with the mouse.

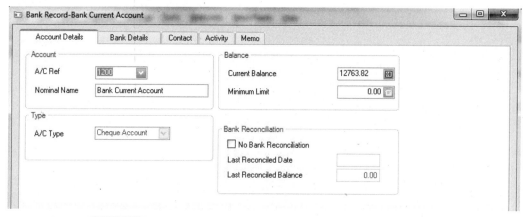

Choose the Activity tab at the top.

KAPLAN PUBLISHING

You should now see the following screen.

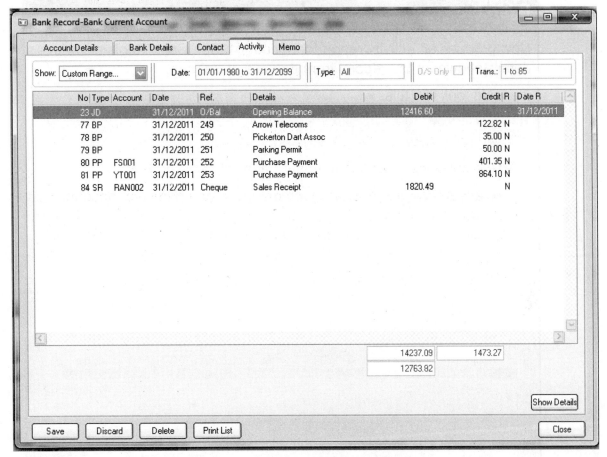

This shows all the transactions to date affecting N/C 1200 (the main current account). Make sure you can identify all of these.

Further details of individual transactions can be obtained by clicking on the Show Details button as shown in Exercise overleaf.

Note that Debit entries represent monies paid **into** the bank account; credit entries show payments **out of** the bank account.

Exercise

Now produce an activity report for account 1235 ('Cash Register') with details shown for the receipt from the sale of trainers.

It should look like this:

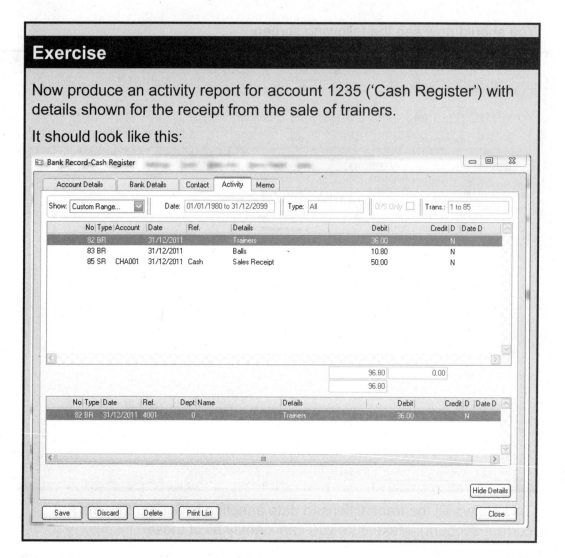

Exercise

You should now produce a revised Trial Balance.

Your Trial Balance should now look like this.

TotalPhotoLtd

Period Trial Balance

Date: 28/10/2011	**Wynn Bowlden Tennis Coach**	Page: 1
Time: 09:00:47	**Period Trial Balance**	

To Period: Month 12, December 2011

N/C	Name	Debit	Credit
0030	Office Equipment	3,420.00	
0031	Office Equipment Depreciation		1,710.00
0050	Motor Vehicles	8,000.00	
0051	Motor Vehicles Depreciation		2,000.00
1001	Stock	2,865.90	
1100	Debtors Control Account	2,299.21	
1200	Bank Current Account	12,763.82	
1230	Petty Cash	100.00	
1235	Cash Register	96.80	
2100	Creditors Control Account		3,827.90
2200	Sales Tax Control Account		159.47
2201	Purchase Tax Control Account	167.35	
2202	VAT Liability		981.61
3000	Capital		3,500.00
3200	Profit and Loss Account		4,121.14
4000	Sales - Equipment		2,025.53
4001	Sales - Clothing and Footwear		2,283.79
4002	Sales - Individual Coaching		13,469.30
4003	Sales - Group Coaching		13,910.50
4004	Sales - Other		601.60
5000	Purchases - Equipment	1,254.70	
5001	Purchases - Clothing and Footwear	1,618.90	
5002	Purchases - Stationery	601.79	
5003	Purchases - Packaging	208.78	
5004	Purchases - Other Consumables	104.61	
6201	Advertising	35.00	
7100	Rent	3,600.00	
7103	General Rates	350.00	
7304	Miscellaneous Motor Expenses	8,654.47	
7502	Telephone	593.87	
8207	General Expenses	1,855.64	
	Totals:	48,590.84	48,590.84

12 Transfers

Sometimes a business may transfer money from one account to another. For example, it may transfer money from 'Cash Register' to the 'Current Bank Account'. Alternatively, it may transfer an amount from the current account to a deposit account. It may also need to reimburse the petty cash account with money from the current account or cash in hand.

From the **Bank** module click the icon.

Transfer

Wynn Bowlden operates a petty cash tin, to be used for items such as stamps, milk, tea, coffee, taxi fares etc.

An *IMPREST* system is operated, with an imprest amount of £100. However, it decides that this is too low an amount and so decides to reduce the imprest amount to £200. It therefore takes £100 from the bank current account and puts it in the petty cash tin.

You should enter the details of this transfer as below and then **Save.**

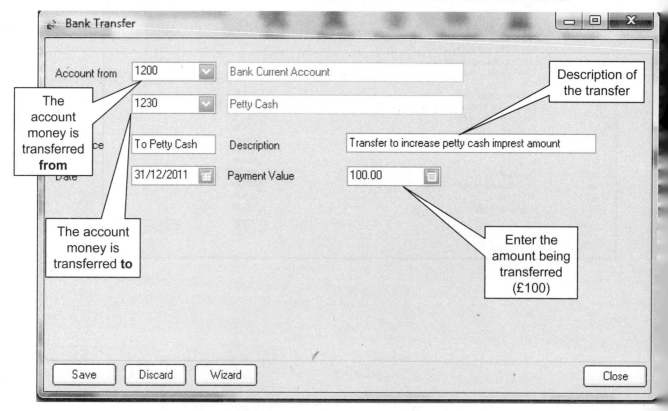

13 Recurring transactions

A business will often also have recurring transactions, such as standing orders or direct debits. These represent regular payments in to or out of a bank account. SAGE allows you to set these up so that you do not have to enter them each month.

On 1st September, Wynn Bowlden signs a contract to advertise on North East Radio for the next twelve months. The cost for this is £120 plus VAT per month. This will be collected by direct debit from the main current bank account, with the first payment being taken on 31st September, and on the 30th of each month after that.

To enter this into SAGE as a recurring transaction, click the Recurring icon from the **Bank** module. Click Add to enter a new recurring entry. Now enter the details of the transaction as overleaf.

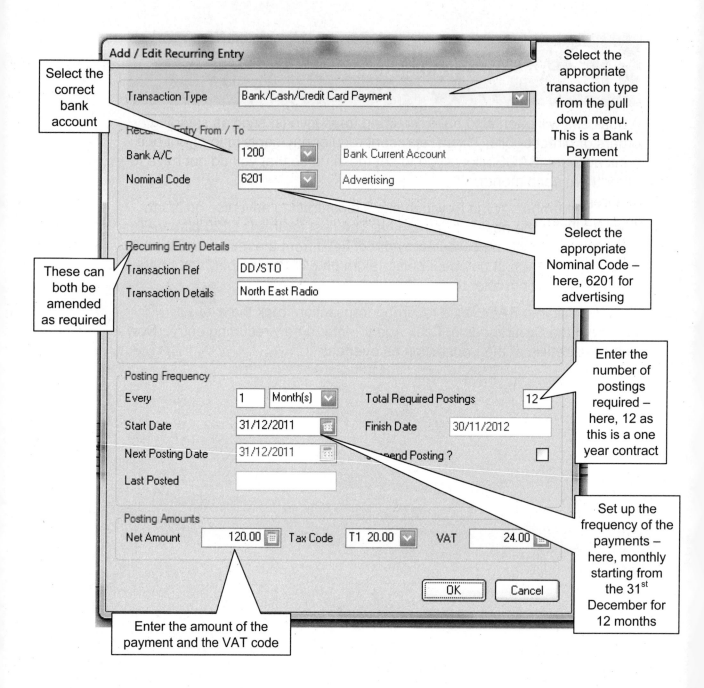

Select the correct bank account

Select the appropriate transaction type from the pull down menu. This is a Bank Payment

Add / Edit Recurring Entry

Transaction Type   Bank/Cash/Credit Card Payment

Recurring Entry From / To

Bank A/C   1200   Bank Current Account
Nominal Code   6201   Advertising

Select the appropriate Nominal Code – here, 6201 for advertising

These can both be amended as required

Recurring Entry Details

Transaction Ref   DD/STO
Transaction Details North East Radio

Enter the number of postings required – here, 12 as this is a one year contract

Posting Frequency

Every   1   Month(s)   Total Required Postings   12
Start Date   31/12/2011   Finish Date   30/11/2012
Next Posting Date 31/12/2011   Suspend Posting ?
Last Posted

Posting Amounts

Net Amount   120.00   Tax Code   T1 20.00   VAT   24.00

OK   Cancel

Set up the frequency of the payments – here, monthly starting from the 31st December for 12 months

Enter the amount of the payment and the VAT code

KAPLAN PUBLISHING

Now that you have set up the recurring entry for these payments, you will still need to post them. This is done by clicking on the [Process] button and then amending the date as necessary.

For now, post the first four month's payments by changing the date to 31st March 2012. Press the TAB key on the keyboard and SAGE will bring up the first four months' payments (December, January, February, March).

Click the [Post] button to post these items to SAGE.

As three of these months fall outside the current financial year (which ends on 31st December 2011) SAGE will check with you that you want to continue. Click yes.

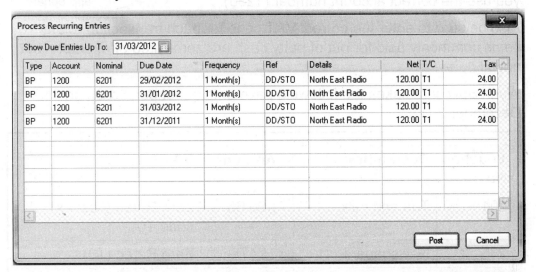

These items are now posted – of course you would need to remember to post the remaining transactions in April 2012. However, SAGE will remind you when you load up the program if there are any outstanding recurring entries to post.

14 Petty cash

Most businesses use petty cash as a way of paying for minor expenses such as taxi fares, tea, milk and coffee, window cleaning etc. We have already seen that Wynn Bowlden operate a petty cash tin with an imprest amount of £200.

Payments out of petty cash are recorded in exactly the same way as any other payments made from a bank account. Remember to make sure that you use the correct account number (1230).

Also be sure to enter the correct VAT code for each transaction. Many items commonly paid for out of petty cash are zero-rated or exempt – but not all.

Wynn Bowlden makes the following payments out of petty cash on 31st December 2011.

Voucher No	Description	Amount	VAT?
204	Tea and milk	£3.65	Zero Rated (use tax code T0)
205	Newspapers	£4.00	Zero Rated (T0)
206	Stamps	£5.60	Exempt (T2)
207	Bus Fare	£5.00	Exempt (T2)
208	Pens	£2.99	Inclusive at 17.5%

Enter these by clicking on the button.

Make sure that the account selected is 1230 – petty cash.

Enter each of the transactions above.

Your screen should look like this:

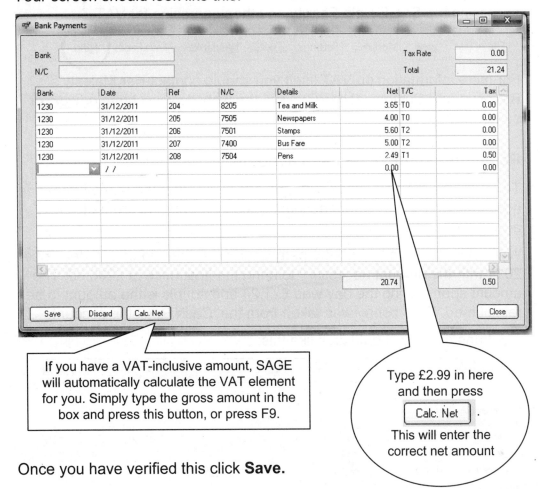

If you have a VAT-inclusive amount, SAGE will automatically calculate the VAT element for you. Simply type the gross amount in the box and press this button, or press F9.

Type £2.99 in here and then press

Calc. Net

This will enter the correct net amount

Once you have verified this click **Save**.

A word about VAT

Value Added Tax (VAT) is a tax imposed on consumers. Whilst you do not need to understand fully at this stage the intricacies of VAT you should have an awareness of the different rates which can be applied.

Most goods and services are taxed at the **STANDARD** rate of VAT (currently 20%). In SAGE, these transactions are given a tax code of T1.

Some goods and services are completely **EXEMPT** from VAT – such as postage stamps. These are given a tax code of T2.

A limited number of goods and services are taxable under VAT, but are currently taxed at 0% – these are **ZERO-RATED**. These are given a tax code of T0. Examples include some food and drink, children's clothes and newspapers.

There are other variations to tax codes and SAGE allows you to easily amend the tax codes and rates applied (for example if the government announces a change in the standard VAT Rate).

Further information on how SAGE deals with VAT can be found by accessing the SAGE Help Facility and then searching for VAT.

File   Edit   View   Modules   Settings   Tools   WebLinks   News Feeds   Help

For more information on VAT itself you should contact Her Majesty's Revenue and Customs (HMRC), view the website www.hmrc.gov.uk, or speak to an accountant.

Reimbursing the petty cash account

To reimburse the petty cash account, simply transfer the money from one account (usually the current account or cash in hand) to the petty cash account.

Wynn Bowlden reimbursed the petty cash tin at the end of 31st December 2011 with the amount necessary to bring the float back to £200.00. The amount spent during the day was £21.24 and so this is the amount to be reimbursed. This money was taken from the 'Cash Register' account.

The transfer entry should look like this:

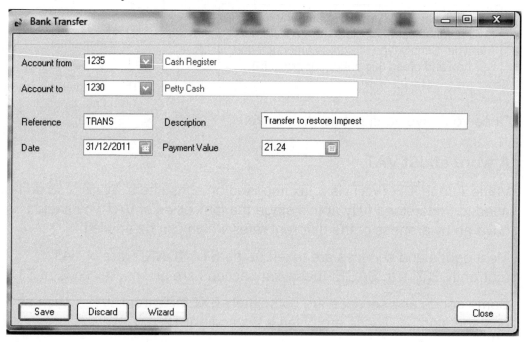

You should now also see that the balance on the petty cash account has been restored to £200, whilst the balance of cash in hand is now £75.76.

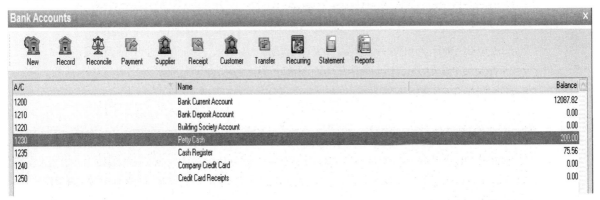

You have now learnt how to process the vast majority of transactions that most businesses will deal with on a day to day basis.

You should now print off a Trial Balance for December 2011, which should look like the one reproduced below.

Date:	28/10/2011	**Wynn Bowlden Tennis Coach**	Page: 1
Time:	10:12:55	**Period Trial Balance**	

To Period: Month 12, December 2011

N/C	Name	Debit	Credit
0030	Office Equipment	3,420.00	
0031	Office Equipment Depreciation		1,710.00
0050	Motor Vehicles	8,000.00	
0051	Motor Vehicles Depreciation		2,000.00
1001	Stock	2,865.90	
1100	Debtors Control Account	2,299.21	
1200	Bank Current Account	12,519.82	
1230	Petty Cash	200.00	
1235	Cash Register	75.56	
2100	Creditors Control Account		3,827.90
2200	Sales Tax Control Account		159.47
2201	Purchase Tax Control Account	191.85	
2202	VAT Liability		981.61
3000	Capital		3,500.00
3200	Profit and Loss Account		4,121.14
4000	Sales - Equipment		2,025.53
4001	Sales - Clothing and Footwear		2,283.79
4002	Sales - Individual Coaching		13,469.30
4003	Sales - Group Coaching		13,910.50
4004	Sales - Other		601.60
5000	Purchases - Equipment	1,254.70	
5001	Purchases - Clothing and Footwear	1,618.90	
5002	Purchases - Stationery	601.79	
5003	Purchases - Packaging	208.78	
5004	Purchases - Other Consumables	104.61	
6201	Advertising	155.00	
7100	Rent	3,600.00	
7103	General Rates	350.00	
7304	Miscellaneous Motor Expenses	8,654.47	
7400	Travelling	5.00	
7501	Postage and Carriage	5.60	
7502	Telephone	593.87	
7504	Office Stationery	2.49	
7505	Books etc.	4.00	
8205	Refreshments	3.65	
8207	General Expenses	1,855.64	
	Totals:	48,590.84	48,590.84

Journals and bad debts

10

CONTENTS

1 Introduction

So far you have learnt how to process day-to-day transactions through SAGE. These have included making sales and purchases and making and receiving payments.

Sometimes, however, a business will need to record an accounting transaction that falls outside the 'norm'. In these instances, a *journal* is required.

Common reasons for journals

- Correction of errors – for example, amending opening balances, removing duplicate entries, or correcting given or your own errors

- Writing off bad debts

- Year end adjustments (e.g. depreciation, accruals and prepayments, closing stock).

2 Correction of errors

You may find that you enter a transaction incorrectly, and post it to SAGE before you have noticed. In this instance you will need to correct the error by producing a reversing journal.

Earlier, you entered a payment from the bank for £35.00 to Pickerton Darts Association for advertising in their handbook.

It has now come to light that in fact the payment should have been for £55.00, the error being due to misreading the League Secretary's rather poor handwriting on the invoice. The correct amount was in fact paid – reference to the cheque stub and the bank statement would confirm this.

The problem

At the moment, the bank balance is overstated by £20, as we have only entered £35 instead of the correct amount of £55. Also, the expenditure on advertising is understated by the same £20.

The solution

You need to produce a journal to correct this error.

From the **Company** module select the icon.

Enter the details as below:

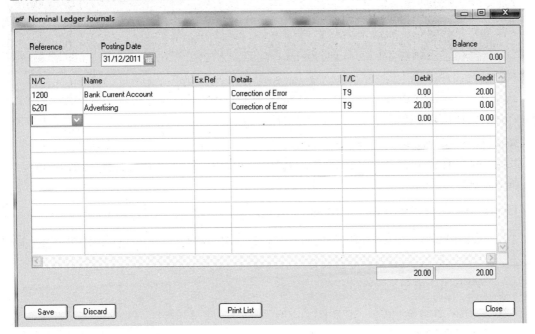

Note the double-entry:

You have credited the bank account by £20 and debited the advertising account by the same amount. Press SAVE.

The corrections function

SAGE also has an in-built corrections function which may be used instead of the more 'traditional' use of the journal.

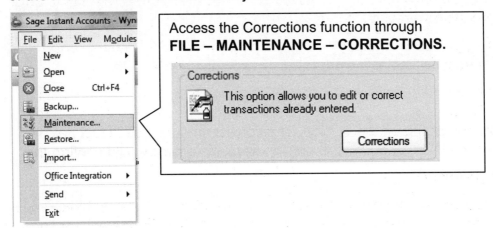

The Corrections function will allow you to correct certain types of errors.

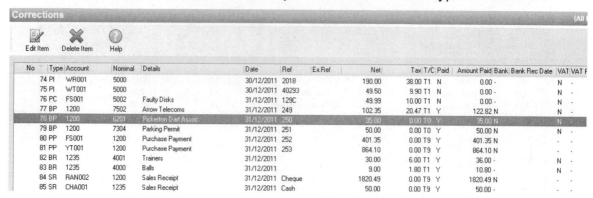

Here, the entry with an error is highlighted. Double click on this:

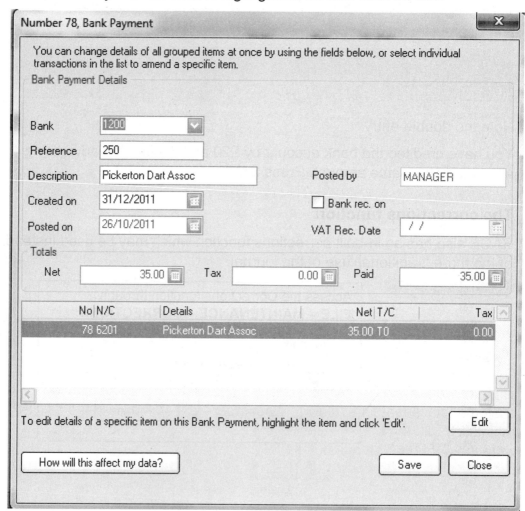

Now you can correct any errors through the original transaction rather than by using a journal.

Note: **If you completed the correction by journal earlier do not complete and save the correction through this screen as well.**

3 Bad debts

A bad debt arises when a debtor fails to make payment on their debt to us. At some point the organization will need to judge that the debt is no longer likely to be recovered and will need to write off the debt. This has the effect of decreasing the total debtors (the sales ledger control account) and creating a bad debt expense that will reduce profits.

To write off a bad debt in SAGE v17 you will need to issue a credit to that particular customer for the amount being written off. The debit entry for this will however be the expense 'Bad Debts Written Off' (already established in SAGE as N/C 8100). This will ensure that the cost of the bad debt is written off against your profits for the current year.

Bad debts and VAT

When a customer purchases goods or services on credit, the supplier will generally charge them VAT on that supply (assuming of course that they are VAT registered and the supplies attract VAT). If the customer subsequently fails to pay for these items it would be unfair if the supplier continued to bear the cost of the VAT. Rules exist therefore to protect the supplier in this case. The VAT can be reclaimed (i.e. offset against a future VAT liability) so long as the following criteria are met:

The debt is at least six months old.

Genuine attempts have been made to recover the debt.

The debt has been written off in the accounts.

Wynn Bowlden is currently showing as a debtor Roland Garros (A/c Ref 2 GAR001). The opening balance on this debt relates to coaching sessions almost a year ago, the payment of which has been in dispute with the customer since that time. On 31st December 2011 Wynn Bowlden decided that it was unlikely the issue would ever be resolved and so decided to write the debt off. The amount is £301.28 (including VAT).

This is processed as follows:

From within the **CUSTOMERS** module, click the **Customer Write Off/Refund** button in the Tasks Bar. Highlight **Write off Customer Transactions** as shown below, and then click **Next**.

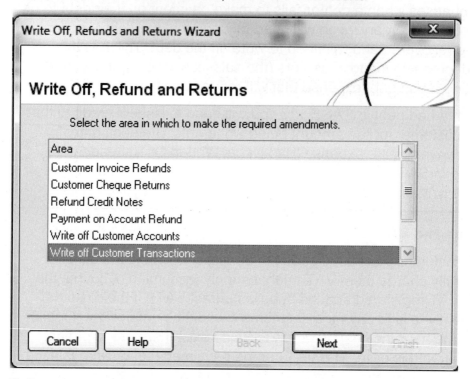

Follow the instructions and select the correct invoice to be written off, as below:

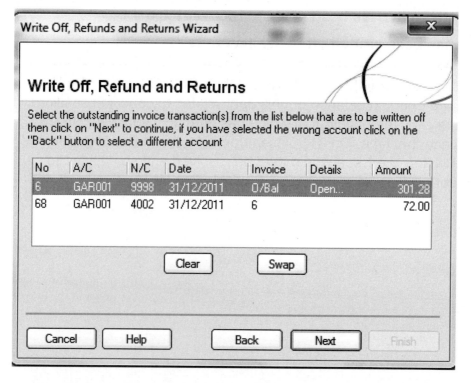

Add a reference and then complete the write-off as instructed:

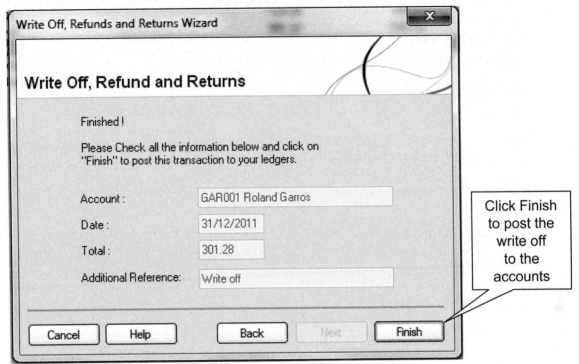

Now you should check the customer record for Roland Garros to be sure that the debt has been written off correctly.

Amending company details and managing data

11

CONTENTS
1 Amending data
2 Exporting data

1 Amending data

As we have already seen, one of the most common ways to correct an error is by means of a journal. This is essentially a book-keeping solution, using a double entry to correct or amend an earlier error. Sometimes, however, it is necessary to change a transaction we have entered that we cannot correct with a journal.

For example, in the Wynn Bowlden Case Study we entered a credit note for a cancelled coaching session. We cannot enter a journal to correct this as Sage does not allow us to post a journal to a control account (the Creditors Control Account). If we needed to correct this simply access the Corrections screen from the tab at the bottom of the screen or from the Tasks Menu:

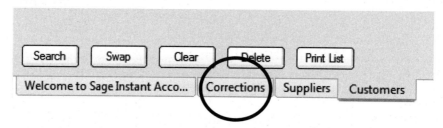

Within the Correction function we have the choice of searching for the item we are trying to correct by many different criteria. One good way to do this is to use the account reference.

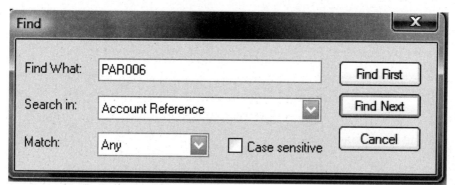

By searching by the account reference of the transaction we are trying to find we can search through the transactions until we find the one we want by clicking Find Next .

Once we have found the transaction we want we have the choice of either deleting or amending the transaction by clicking the buttons at the top of the screen.

KAPLAN PUBLISHING

Pressing delete brings up the following screen:

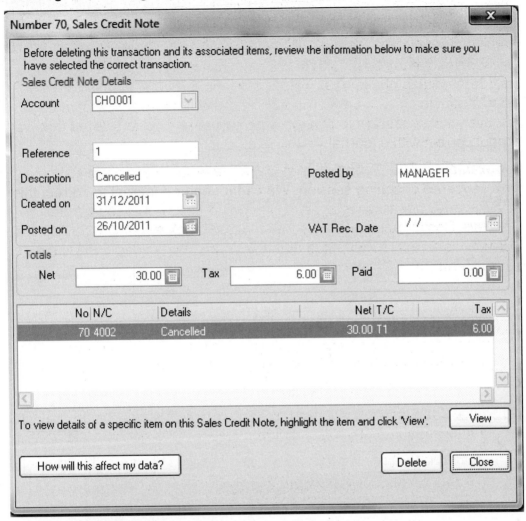

Clicking [Delete] will delete the transaction from the ledger although the fact that it existed will always be shown and it will be offset by a deleting entry as opposed to being completely removed from the ledgers.

Pressing edit brings up the following screen:

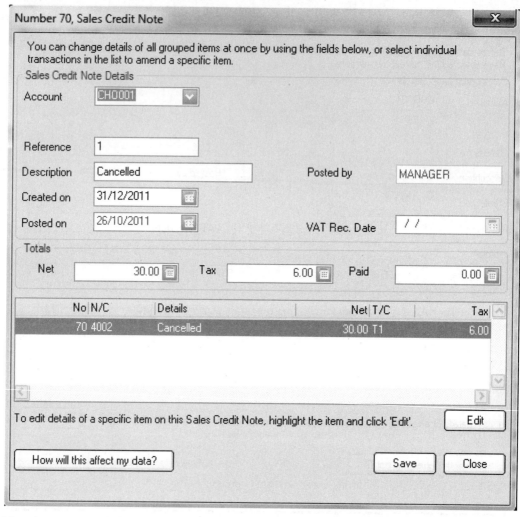

You can amend the details of the credit note from this screen such as the account, description or date of the transaction. To amend specific items (e.g. the amounts or the tax code) you must press **Edit.**

This brings up the following screen:

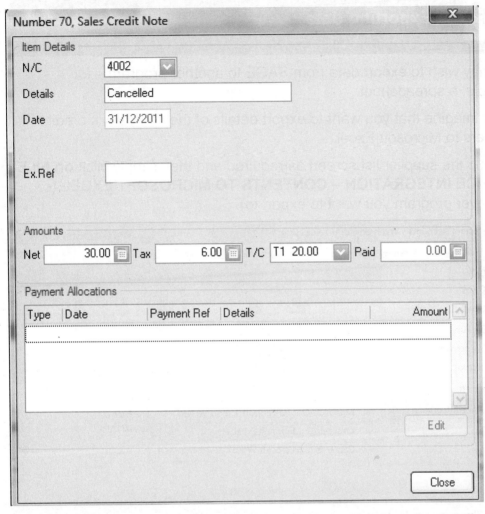

This screen allows you to amend or correct the nominal code, details, net amount, VAT amount and tax code.

Further information on correcting entries can be found through the SAGE help facility.

2 Exporting data

You may wish to export data from SAGE to another program – for example, a spreadsheet.

Let us imagine that you want to export details of the company's credit suppliers to Microsoft Excel.

Bring up the supplier list screen as required and then simply click **on FILE – OFFICE INTEGRATION – CONTENTS TO MICROSOFT EXCEL** (or whichever program you want to export to).

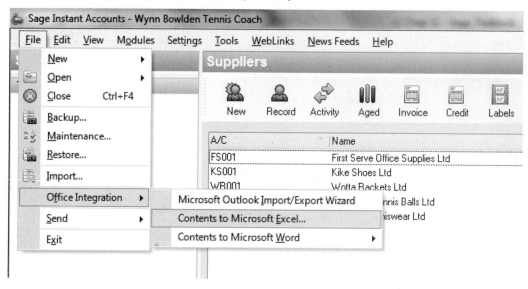

This will export the data to your spreadsheet as below:

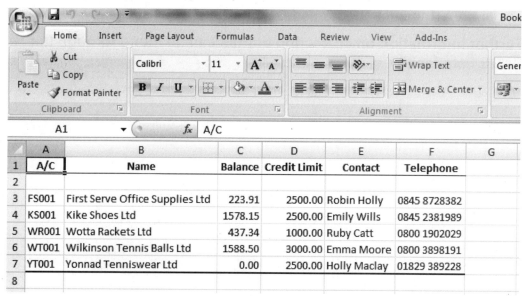

KAPLAN PUBLISHING

Bank reconciliation

12

CONTENTS
1   Introduction
2   Performing a bank reconciliation using SAGE
3   Reports

1 Introduction

A useful exercise for all businesses to undertake on a regular basis is to reconcile their bank account. In essence this means checking the company's own records with the bank statement produced and sent to them by their bank.

Wynn Bowlden received the following statement from their bank.

STATEMENT			
Account number		Date 5/1/2012	
Sort code		Statement No: 49	
Date	Payments	Receipts	Balance
31/12/11 Op Bal			12416.60
31/12/11 Lodgement		1820.49	14237.09
31/12/11 Interest		8.17	14245.26
31/12/11 Cash W/D	100.00		14145.26
31/12/11 Bank Charges	14.60		14130.66
31/12/11 DD	144.00		13986.66
03/01/12 Chq 240	55.00		13931.66

The bank statement will rarely agree exactly with the company's own records, for three reasons:

1 Items on the Bank Statement not yet recorded in SAGE

There may be some items on the bank statement which do not yet appear in the company's records. Here, there is interest which has been credited to the business bank account of £8.17, and also bank charges of £14.60 which have been debited from the account. It is likely that the company would not know the exact amount or date of these receipts to/payments from the bank account until the statement is actually received. Similarly, you should always check that all standing orders/ direct debits / BACS transfers etc have been fully recorded in the company's records. Remember that a 'recurring item' can be set up within SAGE but that these must still be posted.

Discrepancies of this nature between the bank statement and the company's own records should be dealt with by updating the company's records.

You should now enter a **bank payment** to deal with the bank charges and a **bank receipt** to deal with the interest received.

Here is the screen for the **bank payment**. Remember there is no VAT on bank charges (or interest) and so the VAT code should be set to T2 (Exempt).

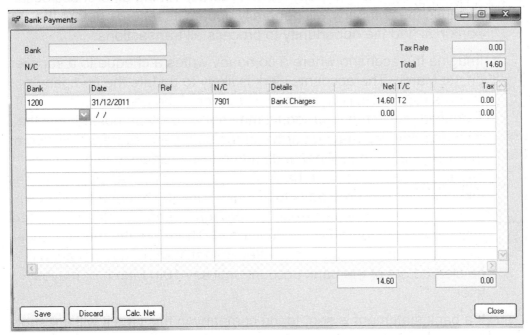

And here is the screen for the **bank receipt** of the interest. Note that there was no Nominal Code for *Interest Received* and so a new N/C has been created (N/C 4906).

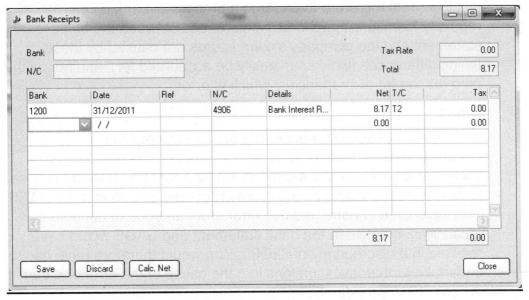

2 Timing Differences

This is a very common cause of discrepancies between the bank statement and the company's own records. Timing differences occur because the company will generally update its records before the bank has had the opportunity to process all transactions.

Imagine the scenario where a company writes a cheque to a supplier on 1st March. The accounts clerk is likely to update the company's records (i.e. SAGE) on that day. However, if the cheque was produced late in the afternoon it may not actually be posted until the following day and may not arrive at the supplier's address until two or three days after that. Weekends and public holidays can delay this further. It may then not be banked immediately by the supplier; it may take them two or three days to actually bank the cheque in their own branch. The cheque must then go through the banks' clearing system which may take three-five working days. Therefore the funds associated with that cheque (written on 1st March) may not actually be cleared out of the bank account until say 10th March or maybe later.

If a bank statement is sent to the company in this time it will not show the cheque payment, as it will not have been fully processed at the time the statement is produced. It will, however, have been recorded in the company's own accounts.

It is important therefore to undergo a process of bank reconciliation regularly to ensure that the only differences between the bank statement and the company's own records are caused by these timing differences (which can easily be accounted for), and not by the third reason for discrepancies, which is error.

3 Errors

It is perfectly possible for either the bank or (more likely) the company to have made an error in the course of producing their figures. We have already seen that the payment that was made to the Darts Association was incorrectly recorded as £35 instead of £55. You have already corrected this error, but had you not done so the reconciliation between the bank statement and SAGE would have resulted in a discrepancy of £20.00. You would therefore have had to undertake further investigations into the cause of the error and then to correct it appropriately.

2 Performing a bank reconciliation using SAGE

From the **BANK** Module select the appropriate bank account and then click on the 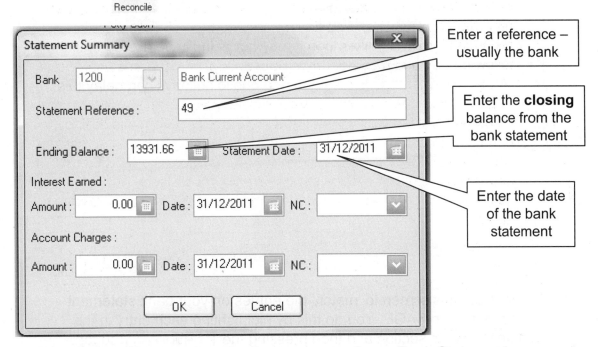 button.

Enter a reference – usually the bank

Enter the **closing** balance from the bank statement

Enter the date of the bank statement

This screen allows you to enter the summary of your Bank Statement. Notice that you can also enter the interest earned and any bank charges directly via this screen as well (rather than entering them separately as bank payments and receipts as you did earlier).

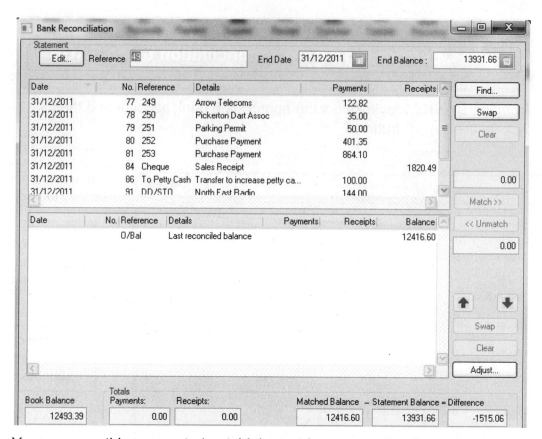

You now use this screen to 'match' the entries on your bank statement with the entries in SAGE. You do this by highlighting each entry in the Unmatched Items section and then pressing the | Match >> | button.

ONLY match the items that appear on your bank statement

You should find the following items on the bank statement and show them as 'matched'

Payment of £55.00 (cheque 250) – *in SAGE this shows as a payment of £35.00 and a journal entry of £20.00; you should 'match' both of these items.*

Lodgement of £1820.49

Bank interest of £8.17

Bank charges of £14.60

Direct Debit to North East Radio of £144.00

Once you have matched all items they will appear in the 'Matched Against Statement' box as shown below:

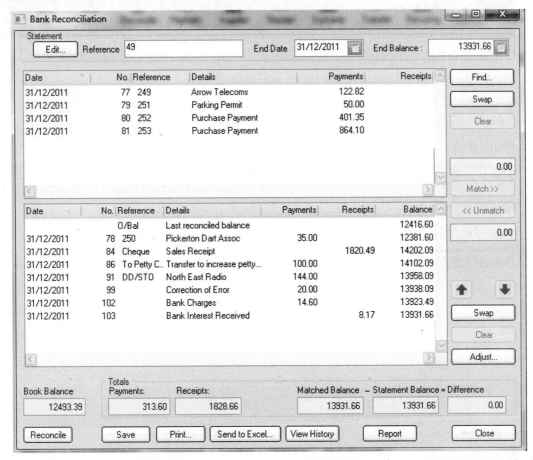

You can see here that the items which appear on the bank statement have now been matched. The matched balance now equals the statement balance and therefore the difference is zero. This is what you should be aiming for.

You should now press the [Reconcile] button to complete the process.

3 Reports

Once you have reconciled the bank statement you should produce the following reports from within Report Browser:

BANKREC.report shows the list of matched and reconciled items within SAGE. (Contained in the **Reconciled Transactions folder.**)

BNKUPAY.srt shows the list of unreconciled payments – these are the payments that you have recorded in SAGE but which do not yet appear on the latest bank statement. (Contained in the **Unreconciled Transactions folder.**)

You should produce and print each of these reports now.

BANKREC.report

Date:	28/10/2011					**Wynn Bowlden Tennis Coach**			Page:	1
Time:	12:08:56					**Bank Reconciled Transactions**				

Bank Reconciled On: 31/12/2011

No	Type	Date	A/C	N/C	Dept	Ref	Details	Net	Tax	T/C
23	JD	31/12/2011	1200	1200	0	O/Bal	Opening Balance	12,416.60	0.00	T9
78	BP	31/12/2011	1200	6201	0	250	Pickerton Dart Assoc	35.00	0.00	T0
84	SR	31/12/2011	RAN002	1200	0	Cheque	Sales Receipt	1,820.49	0.00	T9
86	JC	31/12/2011	1200	1200	0	To Petty Cash	Transfer to increase petty	100.00	0.00	T9
91	BP	31/12/2011	1200	6201	0	DD/STO	North East Radio	120.00	24.00	T1
99	JC	31/12/2011	1200	1200	0		Correction of Error	20.00	0.00	T9
102	BP	31/12/2011	1200	7901	0		Bank Charges	14.60	0.00	T2
103	BR	31/12/2011	1200	4906	0		Bank Interest Received	8.17	0.00	T2

BNKUPAY.report

Date:	28/10/2011			**Wynn Bowlden Tennis Coach**			Page:	1
Time:	12:12:15			**Unreconciled Payments**				

Date From:	01/01/1980				Bank From:	1200
DateTo:	31/12/2019				Bank To:	1200

Transaction From:	1
Transaction To:	99,999,999

Bank	1200		**Bank Account Name**	Bank Current Account	Currency	Pound Sterling

No	Type	Date	Ref	Details	Amount	£
77	BP	31/12/2011	249	Arrow Telecoms		122.82
79	BP	31/12/2011	251	Parking Permit		50.00
80	PP	31/12/2011	252	Purchase Payment		401.35
81	PP	31/12/2011	253	Purchase Payment		864.10
88	BP	29/02/2012	DD/STO	North East Radio		144.00
89	BP	31/01/2012	DD/STO	North East Radio		144.00
90	BP	31/03/2012	DD/STO	North East Radio		144.00
				Total £		1,870.27

These unreconciled payments will appear on future bank statements, when they will then be matched in a future reconciliation.

Health and safety

13

CONTENTS

1   Introduction
2   Risks of using a computerised accounting system

1 Introduction

For your assessment, you may need to display an awareness of health and safety issues when using a computer system.

2 Risks of using a computerised system

Computerised accounting systems may offer a lot of advantages to businesses, but organisations must also be aware of the potential risks posed by such systems. These risks can be categorised as:

- **Physical risks** – caused by system failure, theft, damage or loss or corruption of data, and access to systems or data by unauthorised users

- **Virus threats** – the risk of a computer virus (or similar) being introduced to a network, with the resultant loss of or damage to data

- **Legal threats** – from contravention of legislation such as the Data Protection Act (1998) by an organisation in the way that it stores or uses personal data.

Accounting data is particularly at risk, because it is highly confidential and potentially highly valuable to other people. Hence you must remain especially vigilant to risks to data security.

KAPLAN PUBLISHING

Types of risk

Physical Risks

Risk	Possible Safeguards
Damage from spillage (e.g. liquid)	• No food or drink permitted near computer workstations
Electrical connections becoming worn or damaged	• Keep workstations and desks tidy, with all cabling carefully and tidily arranged • Avoid overloading circuits by plugging too many plugs into a socket or adaptor • Carry out regular visual checks for frayed cables, exposed wires etc. Report any incidences that you find
Theft of computer hardware	• Hardware may be fastened to desks etc (although it may still be possible to open the casing to remove hard drives) • Regular physical checks of IT equipment to ensure the actual equipment matches that held on the Fixed Asset Register • Use of bar-codes and other identifying details to ensure that any items stolen can be quickly returned if found
Damage to, or loss of, memory devices (e.g. disks, USB pen drives)	• Treat all storage devices with care. Although modern devices are quite durable, they can still be scratched or damaged. Even grease left by fingerprints can damage the effectiveness of the disk. • Avoid exposure to devices which contain large magnets – this can corrupt data on the storage device

	• Be extremely vigilant if you are taking memory devices with you out of the office – to work at home or on the train, for example. There are many examples of instances where highly confidential data has been lost in this way. Remember, the data on the disk is usually far more valuable than the device itself
	• Take regular backups of data which are named appropriately and stored off-site in secure storage.
'Prying eyes' – unauthorised viewing of confidential information by colleagues, clients or others	• Remember, if you can see confidential information on your computer screen, others may be able to as well. Angle your screen and arrange your workspace to minimise the risk of other people seeing your work.
	• Always log out of a program if you are leaving your desk
	• Do not leave confidential papers on your desk. Be especially wary if there are people other than colleagues in your office
	• Use a password to protect access to your computer, and make sure that the program automatically logs you out after a few minutes of inactivity

Virus threats

All computers that are linked to 'the outside world' (e.g. via a network or to the internet) are susceptible to security threats. Many people are familiar with the threat posed by viruses or other similar threats.

A virus is a piece of software that is used to maliciously infect your computer. What is more, it then has the ability to replicate itself and infect any other computer that is connected to yours. Of course, this also means that your computer is at risk of being infected by other computers as well.

Introduction of the virus to a system usually takes place when you open a file that has been deliberately infected – for example, an email attachment or a web-site, an infected piece of software, or an infected memory device (e.g. a memory stick).

The consequences of being infected by a virus are many:

- Infecting all other computers you are linked to

- Deleting particular files – especially files which are essential to the normal operation of your computer

- Altering files so they are no longer legible

- Slowing down your computer by taking up huge amounts of memory – leaving your computer extremely slow and unable to perform basic tasks

- Accessing your data and sending it to other people

- 'Reading' your passwords for essential sites such as on-line banking – enabling somebody else to access your bank account

- Wiping your hard-drive – essentially deleting everything from the computer.

Safeguards against viruses

Firewalls: These are designed to prevent 'hackers' gaining access to a computer network via the phone line. These can be a piece of software (now often built in to operating systems such as Windows) or a hardware firewall, which is essentially a box which acts as a barrier between the modem (the phone line into your computer) and the computer itself. An effective firewall is an essential aspect of computer safeguarding, particularly where users have access to the internet.

Effective IT policies: Most organisations now have clearly defined IT policies regarding the private use of the internet and e-mails, not allowing employees to install their own software (e.g. games) on work computers.

Using virus protection software: This is the most important method of protecting computer systems. It acts as a guard dog, constantly watching for suspicious files, blocking or destroying them and advising the user that there has been an attempt to compromise the security of the system. As virus protection programs are constantly being updated with details of new viruses, it is essential that it is kept updated and current at all times. An out-of-date program is no protection against the most recent viruses.

Personal vigilance: Be very wary if you receive unsolicited emails from addresses that you do not recognise. Do not open any emails that you are suspicious of – you should report these to your IT manager or your supervisor. However, you should also be wary of emails (particularly those with attachments) from addresses you <u>do</u> recognise – remember, if somebody you know has a computer which has been infected there is a high probability that the computer will then try and attack your computer as well.

Be very careful when accessing the internet. Only use sites you need for work. Be wary of links to other sites that you do not recognise. Again, if you are in any doubt, or suspect that your computer may have been the victim of a virus, inform your supervisor.

Passwords

Passwords are one of the most common – and most abused – forms of computer security. In most businesses the access to each computer is protected by a password, as well as access to different pieces of software. Even individual files and documents can and should be protected if they contain confidential or sensitive information.

The choice of password is very important; you should be able to remember it, but it should not be easily guessed by others. Ideally, a password should:

- Be at least 6-8 characters long.
- Contain a mixture of upper and lower case letters and numbers.
- Not be a recognisable word.

Under no circumstances should you choose something like your own name, you child's name or your pet dog's name – these are far too easy for someone with only a small amount of knowledge about you to guess. You should also avoid obvious combinations such as 'password' or '123456'.

You should be able to remember your own password. Do not be tempted to write it down in your diary, on a scrap of paper in your top drawer, or even on a sticky note and attach it to the monitor!

You should also never tell anybody else your password – even your most trusted colleague. If you do suspect that somebody knows what your password is, you should change it immediately.

Many systems are configured to require you to change your password every few weeks – even if yours is not, this is good practice.

Backups

Occasionally data is lost, whether through an unforeseen circumstance such as a fire or through computer failure. It is therefore essential that organisations take appropriate steps to minimise the risk of data loss, and to minimise the impact of data loss if it does happen.

Backups should be taken on a regular basis, and at least once a day in most businesses. In addition, individual files should regularly be backed up whilst working on them. There is little more frustrating than spending an hour producing a document or a spreadsheet only to lose it and not to have a back up.

Many programs (including Microsoft Office applications) have an auto-recovery function – essentially a back up is taken automatically every few minutes without the user having to do anything. If there is an interruption or failure (e.g. a power cut) only a small amount of work would be lost, and the affected file can very quickly and easily be recovered.

Copies of backups should be kept securely to prevent unauthorised access or accidental damage. It is good practice to keep a back up at a secondary location (i.e. off site). This way, if there is a fire or a burglary the backup data will not be destroyed or stolen. Some businesses may still take physical backups off site (such as a CD), but this increases the risk of that back up being lost or stolen while away from the office. It is becoming increasingly common for organisations to pay an IT company to keep remote backups electronically.

The Data Protection Act (1998)

The Data Protection Act (DPA) is designed to protect the rights of the individual whose personal data is held and used by other people or organisations.

Personal data are defined in the DPA as:

"data which relate to a living individual who can be identified:

- from those data or

- from those data and other information which is in the possession of, or likely to come into the possession of, the *data controller* and includes any expression of opinion about the individual and any indication of the intentions of the data controller or any other person in respect of the individual"

The data controller is a person who determines the purposes for which and the manner in which any personal data are, or are to be, processed.

Example

If you have enrolled at a local college or training provider for a bookkeeping course, you will have been required to complete an enrolment form. The information you will have completed on the enrolment form is likely to have included your name, gender, ethnicity, birthday, address, national insurance number, your qualifications, any health issues you may have, your bank details and so on. It is essential for the college or training provider to have this very personal and confidential information about you to process your application, to secure possible funding and to send you an invoice or set up a direct debit for your course fees.

However, you may then raise the question – what happens to all this information once my application has been processed? How long does the organisation keep the data about me? What else is it used for? Is it sold to any external bodies (e.g. for marketing purposes)?

These questions (and more) are addressed by the Data Protection Act.

The Data Protection Act has **EIGHT PRINCIPLES**, which state that personal data must be:

1 Processed fairly and lawfully

2 Obtained for specified and lawful purposes

3 Adequate, relevant and not excessive

4 Accurate and up-to-date

5 Not kept any longer than necessary

6 Processed in accordance with the data subject's (i.e. the individual's) rights

7 Securely kept

8 Not transferred to any other country without adequate protection in situ.

Individuals have a number of rights:

• To be informed of all of the information held about them by an organisation

• To prevent the processing of their data for the purposes of direct marketing

• To compensation if they can show that a contravention of the DPA has led to loss or damage

• To have inaccurate data removed or corrected

KAPLAN PUBLISHING

If the data held by an organisation is *sensitive* then extra safeguards must be put in place. Sensitive data is defined by the act as data pertaining to:

- Racial or ethnic origin
- Religious or similar beliefs
- Trade union membership
- Physical or mental health or sexual life
- Political opinions
- Criminal offences

Data about one or more of these sensitive issues may only be held in strictly defined situations or where explicit consent has been obtained.

You can find out more about the Data Protection Act at

www.ico.gov.uk/for_organisations/data_protection.aspx

Protecting yourself whilst using the computer

In addition to protecting your computer and your data, you should also take care to protect yourself. You should make sure that you follow these guidelines on safe working:

- Make sure that your workstation and chair are correctly set up. The screen should be level with your eyes to aid your posture, whilst your chair should be comfortable and support your back. A well-designed workstation and chair can minimise the risk of issues such as wrist injuries and back and neck problems

- Do not sit in the same position for too long. You should aim to take short frequent breaks if you are working at the computer for any length of time – as a guideline you should consider a 5-10 minute break every hour or so.

- Keep your work safe clear and tidy; be organised and ensure you file papers away safely when you have finished using them.

- Do not have drinks or food near your workstation – accidental spillages can easily happen and can have significant consequences!

- There are no proven links between using a VDU (Visual Display Unit) and damage to eyesight, but if you feel that your eyesight is worsening, or you suffer from headaches, you should consult your optician. If you use a computer screen regularly at work you may be entitled to an eye-test and /or free spectacles, paid for by your employer. If you have an occupational health or human resources department at work they will provide you with more information.

Trial balances

CONTENTS

1   Introduction
2   Suspense accounts and errors

1 Introduction

You have already printed out a number of trial balances for Wynn Bowlden. The trial balance is one of the most useful reports that can be produced by a business, as it shows the current balances on each individual nominal account in the company's Chart of Accounts. The two columns of the trial balance (the **debit** column and the **credit** column) must always balance, and so the trial balance is a really useful and simple way of checking if there are any errors in the accounts.

2 Suspense accounts and errors

You may recall that you began this case study by entering the opening balances for the company's suppliers and customers. This created an error in the trial balance (called the **suspense account**). You can think of the suspense account as being like a cupboard under the stairs where things get put until you know what to do with them. Sage automatically creates a suspense account entry when it is unsure what to do with a particular transaction – for example, because of a coding error.

It is important that you regularly check the trial balance to ensure that there are no suspense account balances.

In the case of opening balances, once the remaining balances for nominal accounts had been entered, the suspense account was automatically cleared.

Of course, it is the bookkeeper's responsibility to clear out the suspense account. This way, errors or uncertainties are dealt with as quickly as possible. The usual way to clear out a suspense account in SAGE is by using a journal (see page 122)

Not all errors will be identified through the suspense account, however.

The following table shows which errors would not be identified in this way:

An **error of original entry**	Where both sides of a transaction include the wrong figure. For example, if a purchase invoice for £33 is entered as £35, this will result in an incorrect debit entry (to purchases), and an incorrect credit entry (to the relevant creditor account), both for £2 less. The total of both columns will be £2 less, and will thus balance – albeit incorrectly.
A **Transposition Error**	A particular type of error of original entry caused by putting two adjacent figures the wrong way round (*e.g. 36 instead of 63*). A top tip here is that any resulting difference will always be exactly divisible by 9.
An **error of omission**	Occurs when a transaction is completely omitted from the entries to the ledgers. As the entire transaction has been omitted, the trial balance would still balance.
An **error of reversal**	When entries are made for the correct amount, but with the debits and credits reversed. For example, if a cash purchase for £50 is debited to the Cash account, and credited to the Purchases account.
An **error of commission**	When entries are made for the correct amount, and the appropriate side (debit or credit), but one or more entries are made to the wrong account of the correct type – for example, the debit entry for the purchase of stamps being made against stationery costs instead of postage.

An **error of principle**	When the entries are made for the correct amount, and to the appropriate side (debit or credit), as with an error of commission, but the wrong **type** of account is used – a common example being to debit an *expense* account (e.g. purchases) with the costs of a purchase of an *asset* (e.g. machinery).
Compensating errors	These are multiple unrelated errors that would individually lead to an imbalance, but have the combined effect of cancelling each other out.

If you discover that your trial balance contains an unexpected error (or non-agreement) you should try to identify why this has happened. To do this you should:

- **Produce a Nominal Activity report** for the suspense account code (9998) – this will provide you with information about the balance on the suspense account.

- **Print an audit trail** of recent transactions – this will show you all your entries which you can then compare to the figures that should have been entered.

Reports

15

CONTENTS

1 Introduction

Although it is possible to create and produce your own SAGE reports, there are a number of extremely useful report layouts already set up.

2 The Audit Trail

One of the most useful reports on Sage is the Audit Trail. This provides you with a full list of all transactions that you have entered. Each transaction is numbered sequentially, with corresponding details such as the date, the type of transaction (e.g. JC = Journal Credit, JD = Journal Debit), any narrative or description you have entered and so on.

To access the Audit Trail enter **COMPANY – FINANCIALS** and then click on the Audit icon.

As with most reports, you can select which level of detail you require (brief, summary, detailed, or deleted transactions), and whether you wish to send the report to the printer, simply to preview it on screen, or to save it.

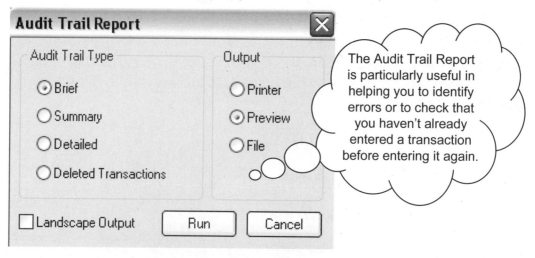

The Audit Trail Report is particularly useful in helping you to identify errors or to check that you haven't already entered a transaction before entering it again.

You can then choose whether to view all transactions, or whether to search by criteria such as date of transaction, transaction number, or by specific suppliers or customers.

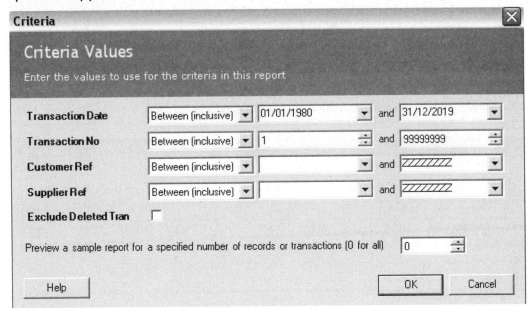

You should note that, as with other areas of Sage, any deleted transactions will be shown in RED.

3 Other reports

You have already seen a number of these throughout the manual.

You should now make yourself familiar with these, plus the other reports shown on the following pages.

Note that there are many other reports within SAGE; you should take the time to examine all of these to find the reports that will best suit your business.

Customer reports

Aged Debtors Analysis (Report CSTAGED.report)

Date: 28/10/2011   **Wynn Bowlden Tennis Coach**   Page: 1
Time: 15:44:09

Aged Debtors Analysis (Detailed)

Date From:	01/01/1980	Customer From:	
Date To:	31/12/2011	Customer To:	ZZZZZZZZ
Include future transactions:	No		
Exclude later payments:	No		

** NOTE: All report values are shown in Base Currency, unless otherwise indicated **

A/C: BAT001   Name: G Bates   Contact: Tel:

No	Type	Date	Ref	Details	Balance	Future	Current	Period 1	Period 2	Period 3	Older
66	SI	31/12/2011	4		144.00	0.00	144.00	0.00	0.00	0.00	0.00
				Totals:	144.00	0.00	144.00	0.00	0.00	0.00	0.00

Turnover: 120.00
Credit Limit £ 1,000.00

A/C: CHA001   Name: Noah Chang   Contact: Tel:

No	Type	Date	Ref	Details	Balance	Future	Current	Period 1	Period 2	Period 3	Older
9	SI	31/12/2011	O/Bal	Opening Balance	59.26	0.00	59.26	0.00	0.00	0.00	0.00
63	SI	31/12/2011	1		70.00	0.00	70.00	0.00	0.00	0.00	0.00
				Totals:	129.26	0.00	129.26	0.00	0.00	0.00	0.00

Turnover: 167.59
Credit Limit £ 500.00

A/C: CHO001   Name: Annette Chord   Contact: Tel:

No	Type	Date	Ref	Details	Balance	Future	Current	Period 1	Period 2	Period 3	Older
7	SI	31/12/2011	O/Bal	Opening Balance	819.20	0.00	819.20	0.00	0.00	0.00	0.00
64	SI	31/12/2011	2		72.00	0.00	72.00	0.00	0.00	0.00	0.00
67	SI	31/12/2011	5		36.00	0.00	36.00	0.00	0.00	0.00	0.00
70	SC	31/12/2011	1	Cancelled	-36.00	0.00	-36.00	0.00	0.00	0.00	0.00
				Totals:	891.20	0.00	891.20	0.00	0.00	0.00	0.00

Turnover: 879.20
Credit Limit £ 1,000.00

*Shows a list of debtors with analysis of how long the debts have been in existence. **Note:** The screenshot above is only an extract of the report.*

Day Books – Customer Invoices (Report CSTDYIVD.report)

Date: 28/10/2011   **Wynn Bowlden Tennis Coach**   Page: 1
Time: 15:46:41

Day Books: Customer Invoices (Detailed)

Date From:	01/01/1980	Customer From:	
Date To:	31/12/2019	Customer To:	ZZZZZZZZ
Transaction From:	1	N/C From:	
Transaction To:	99,999,999	N/C To:	99999999
Dept From:	0		
Dept To:	999		

Tran No.	Type	Date	A/C Ref	N/C	Inv Ref	Dept.	Details	Net Amount	Tax Amount	T/C	Gross Amount	V	B
6	SI	31/12/2011	GAR001	9998	O/Bal	0	Opening Balance	301.28	0.00	T9	301.28	-	-
7	SI	31/12/2011	CHO001	9998	O/Bal	0	Opening Balance	819.20	0.00	T9	819.20	-	-
8	SI	31/12/2011	RAN002	9998	O/Bal	0	Opening Balance	1,820.49	0.00	T9	1,820.49	-	-
9	SI	31/12/2011	CHA001	9998	O/Bal	0	Opening Balance	109.26	0.00	T9	109.26	-	-
10	SI	31/12/2011	LIT001	9998	O/Bal	0	Opening Balance	209.47	0.00	T9	209.47	-	-
63	SI	31/12/2011	CHA001	4001	1	0		58.33	11.67	T1	70.00	N	-
64	SI	31/12/2011	CHO001	4002	2	0		60.00	12.00	T1	72.00	N	-
65	SI	31/12/2011	LIT001	4003	3	0		220.00	44.00	T1	264.00	N	-
66	SI	31/12/2011	BAT001	4002	4	0		120.00	24.00	T1	144.00	N	-
67	SI	31/12/2011	CHO001	4002	5	0		30.00	6.00	T1	36.00	N	-
68	SI	31/12/2011	GAR001	4002	6	0		60.00	12.00	T1	72.00	N	-
69	SI	31/12/2011	RAN002	4003	7	0		240.00	48.00	T1	288.00	N	-
							Totals:	4,048.03	157.67		4,205.70		

Shows a list of all sales invoices produced inc. the Net, VAT and Gross Amounts.

Customer Activity – Detailed (Report CSTACTD.report)

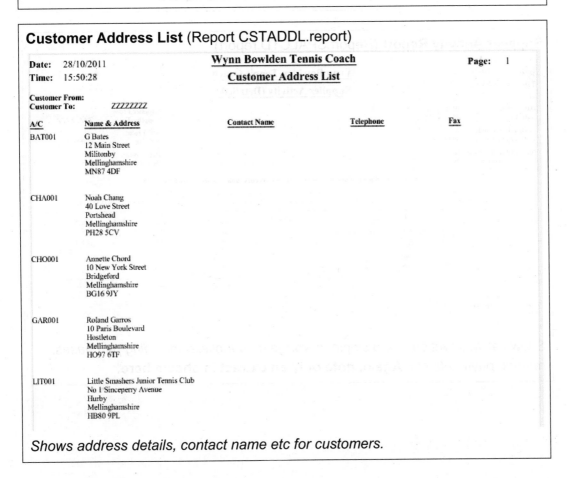

Date:	28/10/2011		Wynn Bowlden Tennis Coach						Page: 1
Time:	15:47:29		Customer Activity (Detailed)						

Date From:	01/01/1980				Customer From:			
Date To:	31/12/2011				Customer To:	ZZZZZZZ		
Transaction From:	1				N/C From:			
Transaction To:	99,999,999				N/C To:	99999999		
Inc b/fwd transaction:	No				Dept From:	0		
Exc later payment:	No				Dept To:	999		

** NOTE: All report values are shown in Base Currency, unless otherwise indicated **

A/C: BAT001   Name: G Bates   Contact: Tel:

No	Type	Date	Ref	N/C	Details	Dept	T/C	Value	O/S	Debit	Credit	V	B
66	SI	31/12/2011	4	4002		0	T1	144.00 *	144.00	144.00		N	-
					Totals:			144.00	144.00	144.00			

Amount Outstanding	144.00
Amount Paid this period	0.00
Credit Limit £	1,000.00
Turnover YTD	120.00

A/C: CHA001   Name: Noah Chang   Contact: Tel:

No	Type	Date	Ref	N/C	Details	Dept	T/C	Value	O/S	Debit	Credit	V	B
9	SI	31/12/2011	O/Bal	9998	Opening Balance	0	T9	109.26 p	59.26	109.26		-	-
63	SI	31/12/2011	1	4001		0	T1	70.00 *	70.00	70.00		N	-
85	SR	31/12/2011	Cash	1235	Sales Receipt	0	T9	50.00			50.00	-	-
					Totals:			129.26	129.26	179.26	50.00		

Amount Outstanding	129.26
Amount Paid this period	50.00
Credit Limit £	500.00
Turnover YTD	167.59

Shows all transactions for customers (e.g. purchases and receipts). **Note the screenshot above is only an extract of the full report.**

Customer Address List (Report CSTADDL.report)

Date:	28/10/2011	Wynn Bowlden Tennis Coach		Page: 1
Time:	15:50:28	Customer Address List		

Customer From:
Customer To: ZZZZZZZ

A/C	Name & Address	Contact Name	Telephone	Fax
BAT001	G Bates 12 Main Street Militomby Mellinghamshire MN87 4DF			
CHA001	Noah Chang 40 Love Street Portshead Mellinghamshire PH28 5CV			
CHO001	Annette Chord 10 New York Street Bridgeford Mellinghamshire BG16 9JY			
GAR001	Roland Garros 10 Paris Boulevard Hostleton Mellinghamshire HO97 6TF			
LIT001	Little Smashers Junior Tennis Club No 1 Sinceperry Avenue Hurby Mellinghamshire HB80 9PL			

Shows address details, contact name etc for customers.

Supplier reports

Aged Creditors Analysis (Report SPLAGED.report)

Date:	28/10/2011		**Wynn Bowlden Tennis Coach**					Page:	1
Time:	15:52:01		**Aged Creditors Analysis (Detailed)**						

Date From:	01/01/1980					Supplier From:	
Date To:	31/12/2011					Supplier To:	ZZZZZZZZ

Include future transactions: No
Exclude later payments: No

** NOTE: All report values are shown in Base Currency, unless otherwise indicated **

A/C:	FS001	Name:	First Serve Office Supplies Ltd	Contact:	Robin Holly	Tel:	0845 8728382

No:	Type	Date	Ref	Details	Balance	Future	Current	Period 1	Period 2	Period 3	Older
72	PI	29/12/2011	309		264.00	0.00	264.00	0.00	0.00	0.00	0.00
73	PI	29/12/2011	312		19.90	0.00	19.90	0.00	0.00	0.00	0.00
76	PC	31/12/2011	129C	Faulty Disks	-59.99	0.00	-59.99	0.00	0.00	0.00	0.00
				Totals:	223.91	0.00	223.91	0.00	0.00	0.00	0.00

Turnover: 587.94
Credit Limit £ 2,500.00

A/C:	KS001	Name:	Kike Shoes Ltd	Contact:	Emily Wills	Tel:	0845 2381989

No:	Type	Date	Ref	Details	Balance	Future	Current	Period 1	Period 2	Period 3	Older
2	PI	31/12/2011	O/Bal	Opening Balance	1,208.19	0.00	1,208.19	0.00	0.00	0.00	0.00
71	PI	29/12/2011	1892		369.96	0.00	369.96	0.00	0.00	0.00	0.00
				Totals:	1,578.15	0.00	1,578.15	0.00	0.00	0.00	0.00

Turnover: 1,516.49
Credit Limit £ 2,500.00

Shows the outstanding creditor balances and how long the debts have been in existence. **Note this is only an extract of the whole report.**

Supplier Activity Report (Report SPALCTD.report)

Date:	28/10/2011		**Wynn Bowlden Tennis Coach**					Page:	1
Time:	15:53:02		**Supplier Activity (Detailed)**						

Date From:	01/01/1980					Supplier From:	
Date To:	31/12/2011					Supplier To:	ZZZZZZZZ
Transaction From:	1					N/C From:	
Transaction To:	99,999,999					N/C To:	99999999
Inc b/fwd transaction:	No					Dept From:	0
Exc later payment:	No					Dept To:	999

** NOTE: All report values are shown in Base Currency, unless otherwise indicated **

A/C:	FS001	Name:	First Serve Office Supplies Ltd	Contact:	Robin Holly	Tel:	0845 8728382

No	Type	Date	Ref	N/C	Details	Dept	T/C	Value	O/S	Debit	Credit	V	B
5	PI	31/12/2011	O/Bal	9998	Opening Balance	0	T9	401.35	0.00		401.35	-	-
72	PI	29/12/2011	309	5002		0	T1	264.00 *	264.00		264.00	N	-
73	PI	29/12/2011	312	5002		0	T1	19.90 *	19.90		19.90	N	-
76	PC	31/12/2011	129C	5002	Faulty Disks	0	T1	59.99 *	-59.99	59.99		N	-
80	PP	31/12/2011	252	1200	Purchase Payment	0	T9	401.35	0.00	401.35		-	N
					Totals:			223.91	223.91	461.34	685.25		

Amount Outstanding 223.91
Amount paid this period 401.35
Credit Limit £ 2,500.00
Turnover YTD 587.94

Shows all transactions for a single, or range of, suppliers, including purchases, returns, payments etc. **Again, note only an extract is shown here.**

Supplier Invoices Due (Report SPLIVDUE.report)

Date:	28/10/2011		**Wynn Bowlden Tennis Coach**		Page:	1
Time:	15:55:58		**Supplier Invoices Due**			

					Date From:	01/01/1980
Supplier From:					Date To:	31/12/2011
Supplier To:	ZZZZZZZZ					
Transaction From:	1				Exc Later Payments:	No
Transaction To:	99,999,999					

A/C:	FS001	Name:	First Serve Office Supplies Ltd	Contact:	Robin Holly	Tel:	0845 8728382

No	Type	Ref	Date	Details	Amount	Paid	Outstanding
72	PI	309	29/12/2011		264.00	0.00	264.00
73	PI	312	29/12/2011		19.90	0.00	19.90
76	PC	129C	31/12/2011	Faulty Disks	59.99	0.00	-59.99
					Total:		223.91

A/C:	KS001	Name:	Kike Shoes Ltd	Contact:	Emily Wills	Tel:	0845 2381989

No	Type	Ref	Date	Details	Amount	Paid	Outstanding
2	PI	O/Bal	31/12/2011	Opening Balance	1,208.19	0.00	1,208.19
71	PI	1892	29/12/2011		369.96	0.00	369.96
					Total:		1,578.15

Shows the list of all invoices due to be paid. **Only an extract is shown here.**

Top Supplier List (Report PI_Topy.report)

Date:	28/10/2011	**Wynn Bowlden Tennis Coach**		Page:	1
Time:	15:58:47	**Top Supplier List - YTD**			

** NOTE: All report values are shown in Base Currency, unless otherwise indicated **

Account Ref	Name	Telephone	Contact Name	Last Inv Date		Credit Limit	Turnover YTD
WT001	Wilkinson Tennis Balls Ltd	0800 3898191	Emma Moore	30/12/2011	£	3,000.00	1,578.60
KS001	Kike Shoes Ltd	0845 2381989	Emily Wills	29/12/2011	£	2,500.00	1,516.49
YT001	Yonnad Tenniswear Ltd	01829 389228	Holly Maclay	31/12/2011	£	2,500.00	864.10
FS001	First Serve Office Supplies Ltd	0845 8728382	Robin Holly	29/12/2011	£	2,500.00	587.94
WR001	Wotta Rackets Ltd	0800 1902029	Ruby Catt	30/12/2011	£	1,000.00	399.34

Shows a list of suppliers in order of value of purchases from them.

Product reports

Product Details Report (Report PRDDETL.report)

Date:	28/10/2011	**Wynn Bowlden Tennis Coach**		Page:	1
Time:	16:00:42	**Product Details**			

Product From:				Category From:	1
Product To:	ZZZZZZZZZZZZZ			Category To:	999

Product Code:	BAZ1	Product Description:		Bazooka			
Category:	1	Nominal Code:	4000		Units of Sale:		
Category Desc:	Tennis Racquets	In Stock:		0.00	Supplier part refn:		
Department Code:	0	Location:	Shop		Supplier A/C:	WR001	
Tax Code:	T1	Selling Price:		80.00	Purchase Price:		30.00

Product Code:	MAX1	Product Description:		Maxi			
Category:	1	Nominal Code:	4000		Units of Sale:		
Category Desc:	Tennis Racquets	In Stock:		0.00	Supplier part refn:		
Department Code:	0	Location:	Shop		Supplier A/C:	WR001	
Tax Code:	T1	Selling Price:		150.00	Purchase Price:		70.00

Product Code:	TUR1	Product Description:		Turbo			
Category:	1	Nominal Code:	4000		Units of Sale:		
Category Desc:	Tennis Racquets	In Stock:		0.00	Supplier part refn:		
Department Code:	0	Location:	Shop		Supplier A/C:	WR001	
Tax Code:	T1	Selling Price:		100.00	Purchase Price:		40.00

Shows full details of products.

Product List by Category (Report PRDLISTC.report)

Date:	28/10/2011	**Wynn Bowlden Tennis Coach**		Page:	1
Time:	16:01:37	**Product List (by Category)**			

Product From:				Category From:	1
Product To:	ZZZZZZZZZZZZZ			Category To:	999

Product Category:	1	Tennis Racquets

Product Code	Product Description	Sale Price	N/C	N/C Name
BAZ1	Bazooka	80.00	4000	Sales - Equipment
MAX1	Maxi	150.00	4000	Sales - Equipment
TUR1	Turbo	100.00	4000	Sales - Equipment

Shows all products subdivided by category.

Bank reports

Day Books: Bank Payments (Report BNKBPD.report)

Date: 28/10/2011   **Wynn Bowlden Tennis Coach**   Page: 1
Time: 16:03:11   **Day Books: Bank Payments (Detailed)**

Date From: 01/01/1980   Bank From: 1200
DateTo: 31/12/2019   Bank To: 1200

Transaction From: 1   N/C From:
Transaction To: 99,999,999   N/C To: 99999999

Dept From: 0
Dept To: 999

Bank: 1200   Currency: Pound Sterling

No	Type	N/C	Date	Ref	Details	Dept	Net £	Tax £	T/C	Gross £	V	B	Bank Rec. Date
77	BP	7502	31/12/2011	249	Arrow Telecoms	0	102.35	20.47	T1	122.82	N	N	
78	BP	6201	31/12/2011	250	Pickerton Dart Assoc	0	35.00	0.00	T0	35.00	N	R	31/12/2011
79	BP	7304	31/12/2011	251	Parking Permit	0	50.00	0.00	T0	50.00	N	N	
88	BP	6201	29/02/2012	DD/STO	North East Radio	0	120.00	24.00	T1	144.00	N	N	
89	BP	6201	31/01/2012	DD/STO	North East Radio	0	120.00	24.00	T1	144.00	N	N	
90	BP	6201	31/03/2012	DD/STO	North East Radio	0	120.00	24.00	T1	144.00	N	N	
91	BP	6201	31/12/2011	DD/STO	North East Radio	0	120.00	24.00	T1	144.00	N	R	31/12/2011
102	BP	7901	31/12/2011		Bank Charges	0	14.60	0.00	T2	14.60	N	R	31/12/2011
					Totals £		681.95	116.47		798.42			

Shows all payments from the chosen bank account.

Day Books: Bank Receipts (Report BNKBRD.report)

Date: 28/10/2011   **Wynn Bowlden Tennis Coach**   Page: 1
Time: 16:04:05   **Day Books: Bank Receipts (Detailed)**

Date From: 01/01/1980   Bank From: 1200
DateTo: 31/12/2019   Bank To: 1200

Transaction From: 1   N/C From:
Transaction To: 99,999,999   N/C To: 99999999

Dept From: 0
Dept To: 999

Bank: 1200   Currency: Pound Sterling

No	Type	N/C	Date	Ref	Details	Dept	Net £	Tax £	T/C	Gross £	V	B	Bank Rec. Date
103	BR	4906	31/12/2011		Bank Interest	0	8.17	0.00	T2	8.17	N	R	31/12/2011
					Totals £		8.17	0.00		8.17			

Shows all receipts to the chosen bank account.

Similar reports are available for cash, and credit card, payments and receipts.

Reconciled Transactions (Report BANKREC.report)

Date:	28/10/2011					**Wynn Bowlden Tennis Coach**			Page:	1
Time:	16:05:07					**Bank Reconciled Transactions**				

Bank Reconciled On: 31/12/2011

No	Type	Date	A/C	N/C	Dept	Ref	Details	Net	Tax	T/C
23	JD	31/12/2011	1200	1200	0	O/Bal	Opening Balance	12,416.60	0.00	T9
78	BP	31/12/2011	1200	6201	0	250	Pickerton Dart Assoc	35.00	0.00	T0
84	SR	31/12/2011	RAN002	1200	0	Cheque	Sales Receipt	1,820.49	0.00	T9
86	JC	31/12/2011	1200	1200	0	To Petty Cash	Transfer to increase petty	100.00	0.00	T9
91	BP	31/12/2011	1200	6201	0	DD/STO	North East Radio	120.00	24.00	T1
99	JC	31/12/2011	1200	1200	0		Correction of Error	20.00	0.00	T9
102	BP	31/12/2011	1200	7901	0		Bank Charges	14.60	0.00	T2
103	BR	31/12/2011	1200	4906	0		Bank Interest Received	8.17	0.00	T2

Shows all bank transactions that have been successfully matched and reconciled to the bank statement.

Day Book: Supplier Payments (Report BNKPPD.report)

Date:	28/10/2011			**Wynn Bowlden Tennis Coach**					Page:	1
Time:	16:06:08			**Day Books: Supplier Payments (Detailed)**						

Date From:	01/01/1980		Bank From:	1200
DateTo:	31/12/2019		Bank To:	1200
Transaction From:	1		Supplier From:	
Transaction To:	99,999,999		Supplier To:	ZZZZZZZZ

Bank 1200   Currency   Pound Sterling

No	Type	A/C	Date	Ref	Details	Net £	Tax £	T/C	Gross £	V	B	Bank Rec. Date
80	PP	FS001	31/12/2011	252	Purchase Payment	401.35	0.00	T9	401.35	-		N
	-		31/12/2011	O/Bal	401.35 to PI 5							
81	PP	YT001	31/12/2011	253	Purchase Payment	864.10	0.00	T9	864.10	-		N
	-		31/12/2011	O/Bal	864.10 to PI 1							
					Totals £	1,265.45	0.00		1,265.45			

Shows all payments made to suppliers.

Day Book: Customer Receipts (Report BNKSRD.report)

Date:	28/10/2011			**Wynn Bowlden Tennis Coach**					Page:	1
Time:	16:07:24			**Day Books: Customer Receipts (Detailed)**						

Date From:	01/01/1980		Bank From:	1200
DateTo:	31/12/2019		Bank To:	1200
Transaction From:	1		Customer From:	
Transaction To:	99,999,999		Customer To:	ZZZZZZZZ

Bank 1200   Currency   Pound Sterling

No	Type	A/C	Date	Ref	Details	Net £	Tax £	T/C	Gross £	V	B	Bank Rec. Date
84	SR	RAN002	31/12/2011	Cheque	Sales Receipt	1,820.49	0.00	T9	1,820.49	-	R	31/12/2011
	-		31/12/2011	O/Bal	1820.49 to SI 8							
					Totals £	1,820.49	0.00		1,820.49			

Shows all receipts from customers.

Unreconciled Payments Report (Report BNKUPAY.report)

Date: 28/10/2011			**Wynn Bowlden Tennis Coach**			**Page:** 1	
Time: 16:08:10			**Unreconciled Payments**				

Date From:	01/01/1980		**Bank From:**	1200
DateTo:	31/12/2019		**Bank To:**	1200

Transaction From:	1
Transaction To:	99,999,999

Bank 1200   **Bank Account Name** Bank Current Account   **Currency** Pound Sterling

No	Type	Date	Ref	Details	Amount £
77	BP	31/12/2011	249	Arrow Telecoms	122.82
79	BP	31/12/2011	251	Parking Permit	50.00
80	PP	31/12/2011	252	Purchase Payment	401.35
81	PP	31/12/2011	253	Purchase Payment	864.10
88	BP	29/02/2012	DD/STO	North East Radio	144.00
89	BP	31/01/2012	DD/STO	North East Radio	144.00
90	BP	31/03/2012	DD/STO	North East Radio	144.00
				Total £	1,870.27

Shows all payments which have not been matched and reconciled against a bank statement.

Nominal List (Report NOMLIST.report)

Date: 19/10/2009		**TotalPhoto Ltd**	**Page:** 1
Time: 21:33:11		**Nominal List**	

N/C From:	
N/C To:	99999999

N/C	Name
0010	Freehold Property
0011	Leasehold Property
0020	Plant and Machinery
0021	Plant/Machinery Depreciation
0022	Photographic Equipment
0023	Depreciation (Photo Eqpmt)
0030	Office Equipment
0031	Office Equipment Depreciation
0040	Furniture and Fixtures
0041	Furniture/Fixture Depreciation
0050	Motor Vehicles
0051	Motor Vehicles Depreciation
1001	Stock
1002	Work in Progress
1003	Finished Goods
1100	Debtors Control Account
1101	Sundry Debtors
1102	Other Debtors
1103	Prepayments
1200	Bank Current Account

Shows all heading codes.

Printing reports – *IMPORTANT*

Businesses find it very useful to keep hard-copy (i.e. printed) versions of their reports. They are useful for future reference, for showing to colleagues or managers and, if necessary, to auditors or other external parties.

However, all businesses must also be aware of the following issues of keeping hard copies. Keeping printed reports takes up valuable space; care must be taken to ensure they are kept free from damp and other factors that could damage them. Businesses must also be aware of the confidentiality aspect; by their very nature, financial reports contain very sensitive financial data which should not be disclosed to people who do not have the authority to see them. The more reports there are, the more likely it is that somebody else may see them, and the greater the storage implications – most businesses use lockable, secure cabinets to file confidential information, whilst bigger organisations may need specialist storage facilities.

Then, of course, there is the cost – both financial and environmental. Paper and printing ink cost money, and so businesses should aim to reduce costs wherever possible. There is also a significant environmental impact to paper wastage and ink use. All businesses –and you – should therefore remember the golden rules of printing reports:

1   **Preview first** – all reports on Sage can be previewed on screen before printing. You should always preview first to ensure that the report you are about to print actually provides you with the correct data

2   **Print only what you need** – there is no point printing 70 pages when you only want one small section of the report. Sage allows you to select by a range of criteria and you should get into the habit of carefully selecting your print range before printing

3   **Draft quality except for final reports** – most printers provide a range of settings for the print quality produced – setting your printer to 'draft quality' means printing will take less time and use less ink. Similarly, print in black and white rather than colour, unless it is a final version for presentation to the organisation's management.

4   **Recycle** – don't just throw paper in the bin – make sure it is re-used (if possible) and then recycled. If you are reusing paper (e.g. as scrap) be wary of confidentiality issues.

KAPLAN PUBLISHING

Following these simple rules should:

1   **SAVE PAPER**

2   **SAVE INK**

3   **SAVE THE ENVIRONMENT**

4   **SAVE MONEY**

Managing VAT and producing a VAT return

Introduction

Businesses must register for VAT if their turnover in any twelve month period is, or is expected to be, above a certain level. In 2010-11 this was £73,000. Businesses may also elect to register voluntarily.

Once registered a business must submit a VAT Return on a quarterly basis to HM Revenue and Customs. This can be in paper format or electronically – although HMRC expect most businesses to submit their return online. With this return the relevant VAT payment must be submitted (occasionally a VAT rebate may be claimed). There are significant penalties for any business failing to meet its obligations under VAT registration, and so it is important that businesses account correctly and promptly for their VAT liabilities.

VAT is charged at different rates:

Standard Rated   20% *(From 1 January 2011 this rose from 17.5%)*

Lower Rated   5% (Certain goods and services such as domestic fuel)

Zero Rated   0% (Including most foods, books, newspapers and children's clothes)

Further details on VAT are available from www.hmrc.gov.uk

Some goods and services also fall outside the scope of VAT and are therefore exempt.

The liability to VAT is calculated by:

VAT charged on sales that the business has made *(Output Tax)*

Minus

VAT paid on purchases that the business has made *(Input Tax)*

Manual reconciliation of VAT liability for Wynn Bowlden

SAGE will calculate the VAT liability quickly and easily, but you should always check the figures as there are likely to be significant implications for the business if incorrect information is submitted to HM Revenue and Customs.

To allow you to see where the figures on the VAT Return produced by SAGE originate from, consider again all the transactions you have entered so far. Some of these will have VAT implications, and others will not.

Firstly, preview (and if you wish print) a **Detailed Audit Trail** (from the

Company – Financials module – press the Audit button) for the period 01/01/2011 to 31/12/2011. This will show you a breakdown of every single transaction that you have entered during this period.

It should look like this:

Date:	28/10/2011				**Wynn Bowlden Tennis Coach**									
Time:	16:15:54				**Audit Trail (Detailed)**									

Date From:	01/01/1980											Customer From:		
Date To:	31/12/2019											Customer To:		ZZZZ
Transaction From:	1											Supplier From:		
Transaction To:	99,999,999											Supplier To:		ZZZZ
Exclude Deleted Tran:	No													

No	Type	A/C	N/C	Dept	Details	Date	Ref	Net	Tax	T/C	Pd	Paid	V B	Bank
1	PI	YT001				31/12/2011	O/Bal	864.10	0.00		Y	864.10	-	
		1	9998	0	Opening Balance			864.10	0.00	T9		864.10 -		
					864.10 from PP 81	31/12/2011	253					864.10		
2	PI	KS001				31/12/2011	O/Bal	1,208.19	0.00		N	0.00	-	
		2	9998	0	Opening Balance			1,208.19	0.00	T9		0.00 -		
3	PI	WT001				31/12/2011	O/Bal	1,529.10	0.00		N	0.00	-	
		3	9998	0	Opening Balance			1,529.10	0.00	T9		0.00 -		
4	PI	WR001				31/12/2011	O/Bal	209.34	0.00		N	0.00	-	
		4	9998	0	Opening Balance			209.34	0.00	T9		0.00 -		
5	PI	FS001				31/12/2011	O/Bal	401.35	0.00		Y	401.35	-	
		5	9998	0	Opening Balance			401.35	0.00	T9		401.35 -		
					401.35 from PP 80	31/12/2011	252					401.35		
6	SI	GAR001				31/12/2011	O/Bal	301.28	0.00		Y	301.28	-	
		6	9998	0	Opening Balance			301.28	0.00	T9		301.28 -		
					301.28 from SC 101	31/12/2011	BADDBT					301.28		
7	SI	CHO001				31/12/2011	O/Bal	819.20	0.00		N	0.00	-	
		7	9998	0	Opening Balance			819.20	0.00	T9		0.00 -		

There should be approximately eight pages in total.

This details, in entry order, every transaction entered, starting with the very first entry you made which was the Opening Balance (£864.10) for Yonnad Tenniswear Ltd, right up to the last transaction (Bank Interest Received £8.17.)

This report also breaks down the VAT element of any transaction.

Working through the list you should now find and identify the following:

VAT on sales

No	Type	Details	Net	Tax
63	SI		58.33	11.67
64	SI		60.00	12.00
65	SI		220.00	44.00
66	SI		120.00	24.00
67	SI		30.00	6.00
68	SI		60.00	12.00
69	SI		240.00	48.00
82	BR	Trainers	30.00	6.00
83	BR	Balls	9.00	1.80
		Total	*827.33*	*164.47*
70	SC	Cancelled	30.00	6.00
		Total	*30.00*	*6.00*

Note: **The numbers in the 'No' column may be slightly different in your report if, for example, you have had to make a correction to an entry. You should still be able to identify the entries above.**

The **Type** in the audit trail helps you to identify what type of transaction you entered. Here:

SI = Sales Invoice

BR = Bank Receipt

These result in an increase in the VAT liability for the business, as it has collected VAT from the customer.

However:

SC = Sales Credit.

Here, these entries represent a reduction in the VAT liability, as in the first instance there was a sales return and in the second instance a write off of a bad debt.

So the total **Output Tax** for the quarter is £164.47 – £6.00 = £158.47.

Now identify the following purchase transactions from the Audit Trail:

VAT on purchases

No	Type	Details	Net	Tax
71	PI		308.30	61.66
72	PI		220.00	44.00
73	PI		16.58	3.32
74	PI		190.00	38.00
75	PI		49.50	9.90
		Total	*784.38*	*156.88*
76	PC	Faulty Disks	49.99	10.00
		Total	*49.99*	*10.00*
77	BP	Arrow Telecoms	102.35	20.47
92	BP	North East Radio	120.00	24.00
		Total	*222.35*	*44.47*
100	CP	Pens	2.49	0.50
		Total	*2.49*	*0.50*

Here, the following Types of transaction are listed:

PI   Purchase Invoice

BP   Bank Payment

CP   Cash Payment

These all have elements of VAT which the business has paid and can now reclaim. However, there is also:

PC   Purchase Credit

This is created because of a purchase return (the business returned the camera because it was faulty). This will reduce the amount of VAT the business can reclaim against its liability

So the total **Input Tax** is £156.88 + £44.47 + £0.50 − £10.00 = £191.85

Using SAGE to produce the VAT return

From the **COMPANY – FINANCIALS** module, click on the %VAT button. This will bring up a window which represents the VAT100 quarterly VAT Return. Enter the correct dates for the return (in this case 1st October 2011 – 31st December 2011) and click the Calculate button.

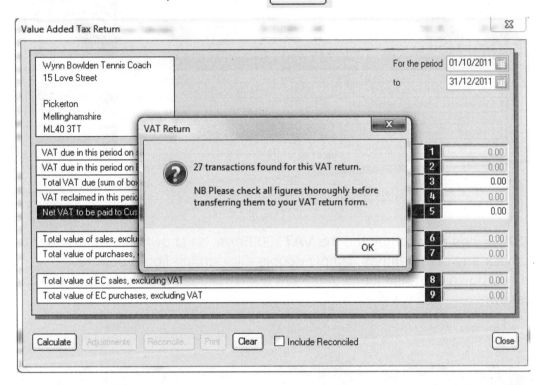

SAGE now indicates how many transactions there are within this particular VAT period and advises you to check the figures thoroughly. Click OK

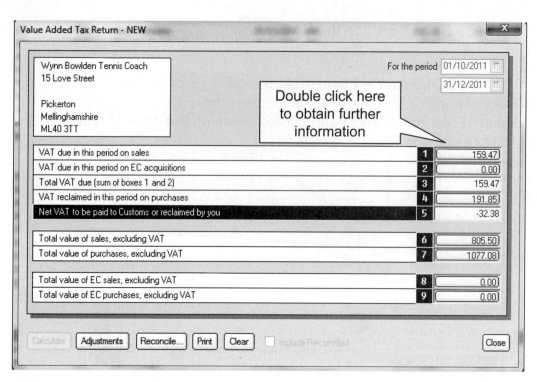

SAGE has now completed the VAT100 Form, as shown above. In order to check any of the entries, simply double-click on the figure and the breakdown of transactions that have been included in its calculation will be shown.

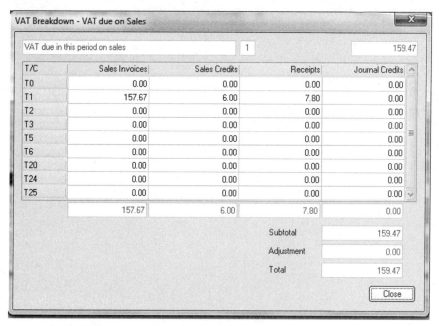

Here you can see the breakdown of figures used – each of these can be further investigated by double-clicking on the relevant cell.

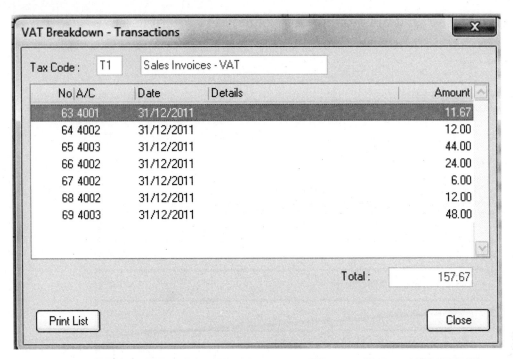

This shows the breakdown of the entries within the figure of £157.67.

You should now check the other entries against the manual check you did from the Audit Trail on pages 168-170. It is also useful to print a detailed report of all the items included in the VAT Return – this is done from the Print Button on VAT Return page. The detailed report should look like this (note this is only an extract).

Date:	28/10/2011	**Wynn Bowlden Tennis Coach**					Page:	1
Time:	16:40:58	**VAT Report (Detailed)**						

Date From:	01/10/2011					Inc Current Reconciled:	No
Date To:	31/12/2011					Inc Earlier Unreconciled:	No

Transactions Included In:

VAT Box   1   Sales Invoice   Tax Code   T1

No	Type	A/C	N/C	Ref	Date	Details	Amount	VR
63	SI	CHA001	4001	1	31/12/2011		11.67	N
64	SI	CHO001	4002	2	31/12/2011		12.00	N
65	SI	LIT001	4003	3	31/12/2011		44.00	N
66	SI	BAT001	4002	4	31/12/2011		24.00	N
67	SI	CHO001	4002	5	31/12/2011		6.00	N
68	SI	GAR001	4002	6	31/12/2011		12.00	N
69	SI	RAN002	4003	7	31/12/2011		48.00	N
						Total for Tax Code	157.67	

Transactions Included In:

VAT Box   1   Sales Credit   Tax Code   T1

No	Type	A/C	N/C	Ref	Date	Details	Amount	VR
70	SC	CHO001	4002	1	31/12/2011	Cancelled	-6.00	N
						Total for Tax Code	-6.00	

Transactions Included In:

VAT Box   1   Receipts   Tax Code   T1

No	Type	A/C	N/C	Ref	Date	Details	Amount	VR
82	BR	1235	4001		31/12/2011	Trainers	6.00	N
83	BR	1235	4000		31/12/2011	Balls	1.80	N
						Total for Tax Code	7.80	
						Total for Vat Box 1	159.47	

Transactions Included In:

You can also print out a paper copy of the VAT return itself:

Date:	28/10/2011	Wynn Bowlden Tennis Coach	Page:	1
Time:	16:43:43	VAT Return		

Date From:	01/10/2011		Inc Current Reconciled:	No
Date To:	31/12/2011		Inc Earlier Unreconciled:	No

Transaction Number Analysis

Number of reconciled transactions included	0
Number of unreconciled transactions included (within date range)	27
Number of unreconciled transactions included (prior to date range)	0
Total number of transactions included	27

VAT due in this period on sales	1	159.47
VAT due in this period on EC acquisitions	2	0.00
Total VAT due (sum of boxes 1 and 2)	3	159.47
VAT reclaimed in this period on purchases	4	191.85
Net VAT to be paid to Customs or reclaimed by you	5	-32.38
Total value of sales, excluding VAT	6	805.50
Total value of purchases, excluding VAT	7	1,077.08
Total value of EC sales, excluding VAT	8	0.00
Total value of EC purchases, excluding VAT	9	0.00

The VAT Return should then be reconciled (press the `Reconcile` button). Reconciling your transactions for VAT sets a flag against each transaction on the VAT Return. This flag indicates that the transaction has been included on a VAT Return, and so is excluded by default from subsequent VAT Returns.

In your audit trail the VAT column shows whether or not a transaction is reconciled. The letter R signifies that the transaction is reconciled; N signifies that the transaction is unreconciled; a hyphen or dash means that it is a non-VAT transaction, default tax code T9, or that its VAT code is one you have indicated is not to be included in calculating the VAT Return.

You have now completed your VAT reconciliation.

Final accounts of a sole trader 16

CONTENTS

1 Introduction
2 Adjusting for closing stock
3 Depreciation
4 Accruals and prepayments
5 Wages
6 Printing the Profit and Loss Account and Balance Sheet
7 Year end procedures

1 Introduction

It is usual (and highly advisable!) for businesses to record their day-to-day transactions on an ongoing basis throughout the year.

When financial reports are produced, however, and certainly at the end of the financial year, there are a number of adjustments that are required to ensure that the financial statements show a true and fair view of the state of the business as at that date.

The most common of these adjustments are:

- Adjusting for closing stock
- Adjusting for depreciation
- Adjusting for accruals and prepayments.

These will now be looked at in turn.

2 Adjusting for closing stock

At the end of the reporting period, the company should carry out a stock take to ascertain an accurate figure for the value of the stock held at that time. This could be one or more of the following:

- Closing stock of raw materials
- Closing stock of work-in-progress
- Closing stock of finished goods.

The process for each is similar.

At 30th September (following a stock take) Wynn Bowlden had stock of £3008.40.

You will notice that this is different to the stock figure that was listed in the opening balances (£2865.90). In this instance, the level of stock has risen by £142.50.

What effect does this have on the accounts?

The increase in stock (£142.50) will have a dual effect.

It will affect the cost of goods sold in **the profit and loss account**.

Cost of goods sold = Opening Stock + Purchases −Closing Stock.

It will also affect **the balance sheet**, as stock is a current asset.

Open up a journal from within the **COMPANY** module.

N/C1001 is the nominal code for Stock – showing it as a current asset. Therefore you need to credit this code with the value of the opening stock (£7403), and debit it with the value of the closing stock (£7208)

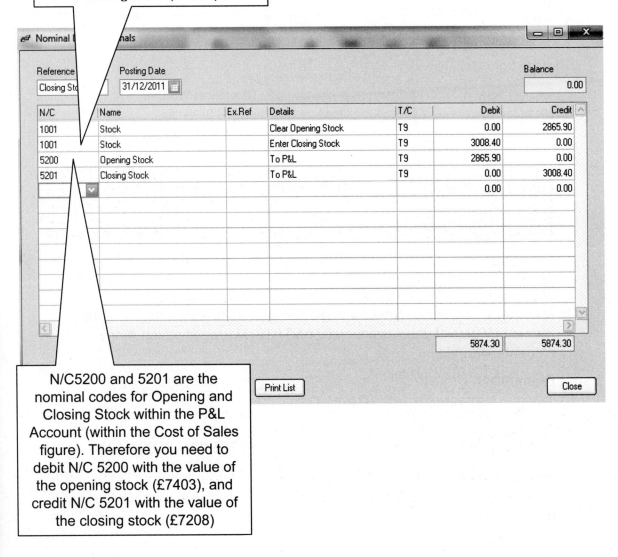

N/C5200 and 5201 are the nominal codes for Opening and Closing Stock within the P&L Account (within the Cost of Sales figure). Therefore you need to debit N/C 5200 with the value of the opening stock (£7403), and credit N/C 5201 with the value of the closing stock (£7208)

You should now check the Balance Sheet and Profit and Loss Account to check that your entries have been recorded correctly:

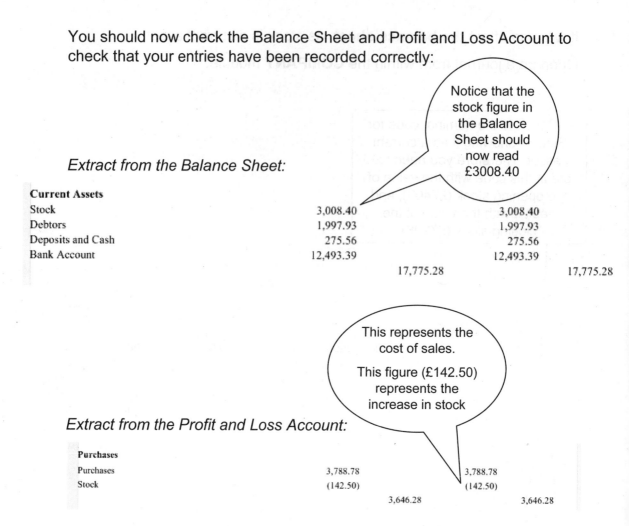

Notice that the stock figure in the Balance Sheet should now read £3008.40

Extract from the Balance Sheet:

Current Assets

Stock	3,008.40		3,008.40	
Debtors	1,997.93		1,997.93	
Deposits and Cash	275.56		275.56	
Bank Account	12,493.39		12,493.39	
		17,775.28		17,775.28

This represents the cost of sales.

This figure (£142.50) represents the increase in stock

Extract from the Profit and Loss Account:

Purchases

Purchases	3,788.78		3,788.78	
Stock	(142.50)		(142.50)	
		3,646.28		3,646.28

Make sure you understand the logic behind this process, as it is sure to form a key part of your assignment and it is an area in which many students struggle.

Remember

> Cost of goods sold = Opening Stock + Purchases – Closing Stock.

In this example, this equates to £2865.90 + £3788.78 – £3008.40 = £3646.28, as shown in the profit and loss account.

KAPLAN PUBLISHING

3 Depreciation

Depreciation is a way of spreading the cost of a fixed asset across its expected useful life – it represents an apportionment of the cost of that asset over the length of time that the company expects it to earn income for it.

The exact method of determining the depreciation expense each year is determined by the company. There are two main methods of calculating depreciation:

- The Straight Line Method

- The Reducing Balance Method

Refer to your most recent trial balance.

To Period: Month 12, December 2011

N/C	Name	Debit	Credit
0030	Office Equipment	3,420.00	
0031	Office Equipment Depreciation		1,710.00
0050	Motor Vehicles	8,000.00	
0051	Motor Vehicles Depreciation		2,000.00

You are advised that Wynn Bowlden depreciates fixed assets on the following bases:

Motor Vehicles   25% per annum on a reducing balance basis

Office Equipment   25% per annum on a straight line basis

You are also advised that no adjustment for depreciation has been made so far this year.

Calculation of Depreciation to be charged

Motor vehicles:

$(£8000 – £2000) \times 25\% =$ **£1500**

Office equipment:

$£3420 \times 25\% =$ **£855**

Having calculated the correct amount of depreciation to charge you now need to produce a journal:

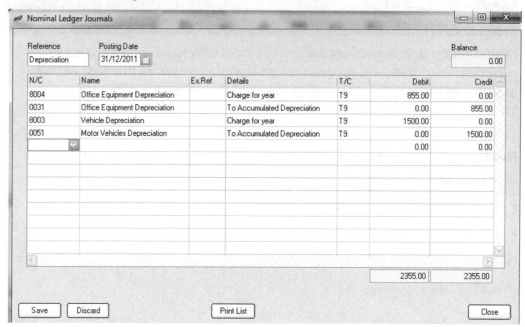

When you have done this you just need to be careful to use the correct code and to use the debits and credits correctly. Remember, you need to **credit** the codes which will appear in the Balance Sheet (because you are reducing the value of the assets) and **debit** the items in the Profit and Loss Account (because you are increasing an expense (and therefore reducing the profit)).

4 Accruals and prepayments

These adjustments are produced at the period end to reflect expenditure or income which has happened during that period, but which relates to a future period. Common examples include payments such as electricity and telephone bills which are typically paid in arrears, or rental income which is received in advance. It is important only to show in the accounts for a period the expenditure or income which actually relates to that period; in other words, if part of the payment refers to a future period an adjustment will have to be made (this is a **prepayment**). Similarly, if we haven't yet received an invoice for something that relates to this period, we will need to make an estimate of the amount spent in the period and include it in this period's accounts (an **accrual**).

Before moving on with this manual you should ensure that you fully understand the principles and application of accruals and prepayments in producing financial accounts.

Accruals and prepayments are created in SAGE using the journals screen within the **COMPANY** module.

Wynn Bowlden has the following accruals and prepayments at 31st December.

Phone   Accrual £40

Rent   Prepayment £100

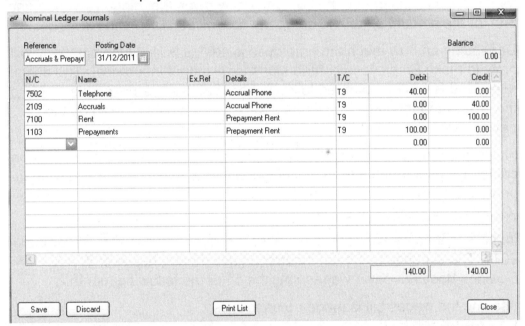

Notice here that Accruals give rise to a current liability within the Balance Sheet and therefore the accruals account should be **credited** (and the relevant expense type **debited**).

On the other hand, a prepayment is a current asset within the Balance Sheet and should therefore be **debited** (with the corresponding expense type **credited**).

5 Wages

When a company employs someone they (generally) must run a PAYE scheme. This is where the company deducts the employee's tax and national insurance from them and pays it over to the Inland Revenue so at the end of the tax year the employee does not have any tax to pay. The wages expense is the debit side of the transaction and the credit side is split into three liabilities, one for the net wages owing to the employee, one for the national insurance the company now owes the Inland Revenue and one for the amount of tax the company now owes the Inland Revenue.

Depending on how much the employee is paid, it is likely the company will have to make Employer's contributions for National Insurance. The actual rules for this you do not need to know here but this is an expense on top of the gross amount of the employee's wages. This will be given on the payroll reports.

Finally there may be other deductions from the employee's wages that the company has to deduct from the wages and pay over. These can include pension payments, attachment of earnings orders and Give As You Earn (GAYE) charitable contributions.

In this scenario we will enter the wages for Wynn Bowlden for December 2011. The expense has been incurred in this month; however Wynn Bowlden does not pay it wages until the 5th of the following month.

Assume the wages bill is made up as follows:

Gross Wages   £1000

	Made up of:	Net Wages	£720
		Pension Contributions	£60
		PAYE	£140
		National Insurance	£180

Employers' NI Contributions   £100

You need to post the following journal:

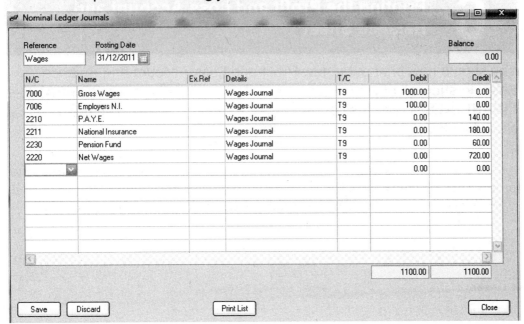

N/C	Name	Ex.Ref	Details	T/C	Debit	Credit
7000	Gross Wages		Wages Journal	T9	1000.00	0.00
7006	Employers N.I.		Wages Journal	T9	100.00	0.00
2210	P.A.Y.E.		Wages Journal	T9	0.00	140.00
2211	National Insurance		Wages Journal	T9	0.00	180.00
2230	Pension Fund		Wages Journal	T9	0.00	60.00
2220	Net Wages		Wages Journal	T9	0.00	720.00
					0.00	0.00
					1100.00	1100.00

6 Printing the Profit and Loss Account and Balance Sheet

You should now print out a new Profit and Loss Account and Balance Sheet to show all of your adjustments. This is done from the **COMPANY – FINANCIALS** screen, using the [P and L] [Balance] icons. The reports should look like this:

Date: 29/10/2011	**Wynn Bowlden Tennis Coach**	Page: 1
Time: 09:43:19	**Profit and Loss**	

From: Month 1, January 2011
To: Month 12, December 2011

Chart of Accounts: Default Layout of Accounts

	Period		Year to Date	
Sales				
Product Sales	32,290.72		32,290.72	
Other Sales	8.17		8.17	
		32,298.89		32,298.89
Purchases				
Purchases	3,788.78		3,788.78	
Stock	(142.50)		(142.50)	
		3,646.28		3,646.28
Direct Expenses				
Sales Promotion	175.00		175.00	
		175.00		175.00
Gross Profit/(Loss):		28,477.61		28,477.61
Overheads				
Gross Wages	1,100.00		1,100.00	
Rent and Rates	3,850.00		3,850.00	
Motor Expenses	8,654.47		8,654.47	
Travelling and Entertainment	5.00		5.00	
Printing and Stationery	645.96		645.96	
Bank Charges and Interest	14.60		14.60	
Depreciation	2,355.00		2,355.00	
Bad Debts	301.28		301.28	
General Expenses	1,859.29		1,859.29	
		18,785.60		18,785.60
Net Profit/(Loss):		9,692.01		9,692.01

KAPLAN PUBLISHING

| Date: | 29/10/2011 | **Wynn Bowlden Tennis Coach** | Page: | I |
| Time: | 09:46:37 | **Balance Sheet** | | |

| From: | Month 1, January 2011 |
| To: | Month 12, December 2011 |

Chart of Account: Default Layout of Accounts

	Period		Year to Date	
Fixed Assets				
Office Equipment	855.00		855.00	
Motor Vehicles	4,500.00		4,500.00	
		5,355.00		5,355.00
Current Assets				
Stock	3,008.40		3,008.40	
Debtors	2,097.93		2,097.93	
Deposits and Cash	275.56		275.56	
Bank Account	12,493.39		12,493.39	
		17,875.28		17,875.28
Current Liabilities				
Creditors : Short Term	3,867.90		3,867.90	
Taxation	320.00		320.00	
Wages	780.00		780.00	
VAT Liability	949.23		949.23	
		5,917.13		5,917.13
Current Assets less Current Liabilities:		11,958.15		11,958.15
Total Assets less Current Liabilities:		17,313.15		17,313.15
Long Term Liabilities				
		0.00		0.00
Total Assets less Total Liabilities:		17,313.15		17,313.15
Capital & Reserves				
Share Capital	3,500.00		3,500.00	
Reserves	4,121.14		4,121.14	
P&L Account	9,692.01		9,692.01	
		17,313.15		17,313.15

7 Year end procedures

At the end of the financial year you need to transfer all of your balances from income and expenditure accounts to the profit and loss account, and then transfer the profit or loss for the year to the balance sheet as retained earnings. All income and expenditure account balances need to be zero for the start of the new financial year, whilst new opening balances need to be created in asset, liability and capital accounts to show the position at the start of the new financial year.

Before running the year end procedures in SAGE you should ensure you have taken two backup copies of your data, and printed all reports you require for the old financial year. You should then set your SAGE system date to the end of financial year date.

Process

Select **TOOLS – PERIOD END – YEAR END**

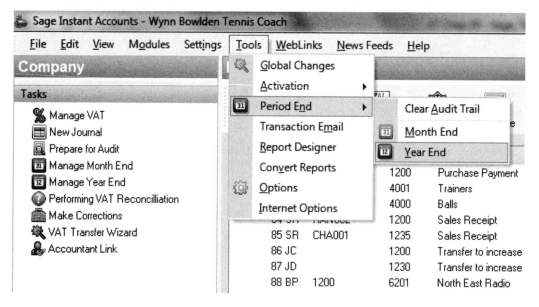

When you run the year end option, your software automatically resets to zero the balances of all your profit and loss nominal accounts for your new financial year.

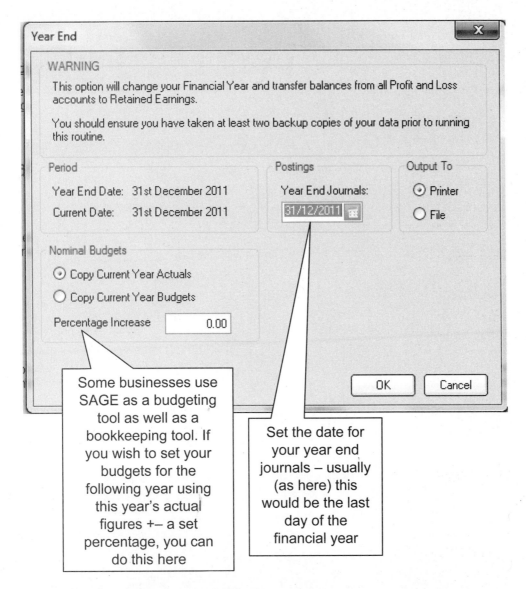

Year End

WARNING

This option will change your Financial Year and transfer balances from all Profit and Loss accounts to Retained Earnings.

You should ensure you have taken at least two backup copies of your data prior to running this routine.

Period

Year End Date: 31st December 2011

Current Date: 31st December 2011

Postings

Year End Journals:

31/12/2011

Output To

⊙ Printer

○ File

Nominal Budgets

⊙ Copy Current Year Actuals

○ Copy Current Year Budgets

Percentage Increase   0.00

Some businesses use SAGE as a budgeting tool as well as a bookkeeping tool. If you wish to set your budgets for the following year using this year's actual figures +– a set percentage, you can do this here

Set the date for your year end journals – usually (as here) this would be the last day of the financial year

OK   Cancel

When SAGE has completed the year end procedure it will print out a report of all the journal entries it has made. You should file this carefully with all other supporting documentation for the year end.

PRACTICE ASSESSMENT

1   Practice Assessment Questions

Instructions to candidate

This assignment is based on an existing business, The ExeFactory, an organisation that makes and sells a range of microphones and speaker systems which it sells to a range of customers. The owner of the business is Simeon Powell, who operates as a sole trader.

At the start of business Simeon operated a manual book-keeping system, but has now decided that from 1st August 2011 the accounting system will become computerised. You are employed as a part-time bookkeeper in the business.

You can assume that all documentation within this assessment has been checked for accuracy and duly authorised by Simeon.

Sales are to be analysed in three ways:

- *Fun and Funky* – a range of cheap microphones and speaker systems ideal for home karaoke machines etc.

- *The Pro Range* – better quality products designed for professional singers and musicians.

- *Cash Sales* – to members of the public at the small factory shop.

The business is registered for VAT, and the rate charged on all items is the basic rate of 20%.

All expenditure should be analysed as you feel appropriate.

When setting the company up in Sage you should select the Financial Year as starting in August 2011. You should set the program date at 31st August 2011.

You should ensure that your name and the date appear on all print outs.

COMPANY DETAILS

Business Name	The Exe Factory
Proprietor	Simeon Powell
Address	10 Topp Way Disclington DS77 9YH
Telephone Number	0845 18090982
E-Mail	info@exefactory.webnet.uk
VAT Number	483876517

Task 1.1

(a) Refer to the customer details below and set up customer records to open Sales Ledger Accounts for each customer. Enter opening balances as individual amounts.

Customer details

Customer Name, Address and Contact Details	Customer Account Code	Customer Account Details
Sunshine Singalongs 10 Pavarotti Way Miltonby MB18 8FC Tel: 01927 21873112 Contact: Chelsea Curle	SS001	Credit Limit = £4,000 Payment Terms = 28 days Opening Balance = £2,031.22 (relates to invoice 00146 dated 21st July 2011)
Carrie Oakey Soprano Avenue Hubley HB2 9GF Tel: 07732 389181 Contact: Carrie Oakey	CO001	Credit Limit = £10,000 Payment Terms = 28 days Opening Balance = £8,143.20 (relates to invoice 00148 dated 27th July 2011)
Poptastic Ltd Caruso Industrial Estate Mellingham ML21 9GF Tel: 07712 381912 Contact: Lewis Welsh	PP002	Credit Limit = £6,000 Payment Terms = 28 days Opening Balance = £4,132.49 (relates to invoice 00154 dated 28th July 2011 for £2,129.21 and invoice 00157 dated 30th July 2011 for £2,003.28)
Sensational Singers Ltd 10 St Bart's Row Kylie's Cross KC19 8HA Tel: 0845 217983 Contact: Dana Miload	SS002	Credit Limit = £5,000 Payment Terms = 28 days Opening Balance = £190.87 (relates to invoice 00129 dated 17th April 2011)

(b) Save your work and print a Customer Activity (Detailed) Report.

Task 1.2

Refer to the Supplier Details below and create supplier records to open Purchase Ledger Accounts for each supplier.

Supplier name, address and contact details	Supplier Account Code	Supplier Account Details
Wardshayne Ltd Unit 72 Killingham KT17 5DE Tel : 02618 1818910 Contact: Majid Singh	WD002	Credit Limit = £5000 Payment Terms = 30 days Opening Balance = £2126.37 (relates to Invoice 189 dated 18 July 2011)
Gates Ltd Birch House Wilchester WL77 4WA Tel: 07715 2781718 Contact: Jeff Little	GT003	Credit Limit = £6,000 Payment Terms= 30 days Opening Balance = £1398.18 (relates to Invoice 18918 dated 20 July 2011)
Young & Co The Lodge Lutton LT54 9PL Tel: 0845 1398232 Contact: Robin Maclay	YG001	Credit Limit = £4,000 Payment Terms = 30 days Opening Balance = £2,101.92 (relates to Invoice YG1089 dated 12 July 2011)
Brooks, Stein & Co 172 Federal Way Herdlington HR89 9WE Tel : 07119 010920 Contact: Katherine Rose	BS004	Credit Limit = £6,000 Payment Terms = 14 days Opening Balance = £1,001.29 (relates to Invoice 7326 dated 20 July 2011)
Lewis Ltd 22 Edinburgh Street Delby DL55 4CH Tel : 01928 238911 Contact: Emily Wills	LL002	Credit Limit = £1,000 Payment Terms = 30 days Opening Balance = £0.00

(c)   Save your work and print a Supplier Activity (Detailed) Report.

Task 1.3

Enter the following opening balances into the appropriate nominal accounts, making any amendments you feel are necessary.

Balances as at 1 August 2011

Account Name	£	£
Motor Vehicles	12,400.98	
Office Equipment	4,219.35	
Plant and Machinery	92,420.12	
Bank	9,218.81	
Petty Cash	200.00	
Sales Ledger Control Account*	14497.78	
Purchase Ledger Control Account*		6,627.76
VAT on Sales		15,212.61
VAT on Purchases	7,524.31	
Sales – Fun & Funky		38,120.19
Sales – Pro Range		29,108.62
Cash Sales		16,210.40
Profit & Loss Account		55,681.39
Capital		25,000.00
Rent and Rates	1,100.00	
Insurance	450.00	
Heat & Light	1729.82	
Advertising	1,480.32	
Purchases of materials	38,734.19	
Stationery	892.36	
Miscellaneous Motor Expenses	1,092.93	
	185,960.97	185,960.97

- *Note:* You do not need to enter the balances for Sales Ledger Control Account and Purchase Ledger Control Account. These totals should already be present as they represent the totals of the individual customer and supplier accounts you entered earlier.

Task 1.4

(a) Use the appropriate software tool to check for data errors.

(b) Print a screen shot of the data verification screen.

(c) Make any necessary corrections.

Task 1.5

(a) Print a trial balance.

(b) Check the accuracy of the trial balance and, if necessary, correct any errors.

Task 2.1

You have received the following e-mail from Wardshayne Ltd (a supplier).

To:	info@exefactory.webnet.uk
From:	majid@wardshayneltd.co.uk

Date: 29/07/2011

Hello

Just to let you know that we are moving! From 31st July our new address will be Blossom House, 87 Thomas Street, Catbury, CT55 3FD

Our new phone number is 0845 6712821

Please ensure that you update all records with this change in address

Kind regards, and thank you for your continued support

Majid

(a) Print a screen shot of the supplier's record with the current address and telephone number.

(b) Enter the new address and telephone number into the accounting system.

(c) Print a screen shot of the supplier's details with the amended address and telephone number.

Task 2.2

Refer to the following sales invoices and credit note:

The ExeFactory
10 Topp Way

Disclington

DS77 9YH

"The Best Microphones, The Best Value"

INVOICE 00160
Tax Point : 1st August 2011   VAT Registration Number: 483876517

Carrie Oakey
Soprano Avenue
Hubley
HB2 9GF

Fun & Funky × 3	£30.00	£90.00
Pro Range × 1	£99.00	£99.00
		£189.00
VAT @ 20%		£37.80
TOTAL FOR PAYMENT		£226.80

Terms: 30 days

The ExeFactory
10 Topp Way

Disclington

DS77 9YH
"The Best Microphones, The Best Value"

INVOICE 00162
Tax Point : 1st August 2011   VAT Registration Number: 483876517

Poptastic Ltd
Caruso Industrial Estate
Mellingham
ML21 9GF

Pro Range × 7	£99.00	£693.00
		£693.00
VAT @ 20%		£138.60
TOTAL FOR PAYMENT		£831.60

Terms: 30 days

The ExeFactory
10 Topp Way

Disclington

DS77 9YH
"The Best Microphones, The Best Value"

INVOICE 00163
Tax Point : 5th August 2011   VAT Registration Number: 483876517

Sunshine Singalongs
10 Pavarotti Way
Miltonby
MB18 8FC

Fun & Funky × 8	£30.00	£240.00
Pro Range × 10	£99.00	£990.00
		£1230.00
VAT @ 20%		£246.00
TOTAL FOR PAYMENT		£1476.00

Terms: 30 days

The ExeFactory

10 Topp Way

Disclington

DS77 9YH

"The Best Microphones, The Best Value"

CREDIT NOTE 41

Tax Point : 2nd August 2011

VAT Registration Number: 483876517

Carrie Oakey
Soprano Avenue
Hubley
HB2 9GF

Pro Range × 1 (Faulty Goods)	£99.00	£99.00
VAT @ 20%		£19.80
TOTAL FOR PAYMENT		£118.80

Terms: 30 days

(a)   Enter the sales invoices and credit notes into the computerised accounting system.

Refer to the following summary of purchase invoices:

Date	Supplier	Invoice No	Gross £	VAT £	Net £	Materials	Accountancy
3/8/11	Young & Co	YG1120	307.89	51.31	256.58		256.58
4/8/11	Lewis Ltd	1918	423.00	70.50	352.50	352.50	
5/8/11	Wardshayne Ltd	218	94.00	15.67	78.33	78.33	
	Totals		**824.89**	**137.48**	**687.41**	**430.83**	**256.58**

(b)   Enter the purchase invoices into the computerised accounting system.

Refer to the following summary of payments received from customers and made to suppliers:

Cheque / BACS Receipts Listing

Date	Details	Customer	£	How Received
04 Aug 11	Payment of opening balance	Carrie Oakey	8143.20	BACS
05 Aug 11	Payment of opening balance	Sunshine Singalongs	2031.22	CHEQUE

Cheques Paid Listing

Date	Details	Supplier	£	Cheque Number
04 Aug 11	Payment of opening balance	Young & Co	2101.92	001301
04 Aug 11	Payment of opening balance	Wardshayne Ltd	2126.37	001302

(c)   Enter the receipts and payments into the computer, making sure you allocate all amounts as shown in the details column.

Refer to the following email from Simeon:

email
From : Simeon@Simeontimbercrafts.co.uk
To : accounts@Simeontimbercrafts.co.uk
Date: 5 August 2011
Subject: Poptastic Ltd

Hi

I'm afraid that Poptastic Ltd have gone into liquidation – I've just had a letter from their administrators. It looks most unlikely we will get anything for their outstanding account.

Please let me know how much they owe us, and then write this amount off as a bad debt.

Thanks

Simeon

(d) Print a customer statement for Poptastic Ltd, showing the balance currently owed. Then make the entries into the computer to write off the amount owing from Poptastic Ltd. Ignore VAT. Print a new customer statement showing the amount written off and the new balance of nil.

Task 2.3

Refer to the following petty cash vouchers:

Petty Cash Voucher

Date 3 August 2011

Ref: PC 22

Details	
Window cleaner (*zero rated for VAT purposes*) Receipt attached	£15.00

Petty Cash Voucher

Date 6 August 2011

Ref: PC 23

Details	
Pot plants for reception	£31.21
VAT	£6.24
Total	£37.45
Receipt attached	

Enter the petty cash payments into the computer. Code the purchase of pot plants to Nominal Code 7803.

Task 2.4

Refer to the following receipts issued for cash sales in the factory shop: you should assume that the monies are banked in the current account immediately.

Receipt	Receipt
No: 369	No: 370
2nd August 2011	6th August 2011
Received by cheque	Received by cheque
£30.00 excluding VAT	£232.65 including VAT

(a)   Enter these receipts in the computer.

Refer to the following email from Simeon:

email
From : simeon@exefactory.webnet.uk
To : accounts@exefactory.webnet.uk
Date: 3 August 2011
Subject: Donation
Hi
Just to let you know that I took £25 out of the bank account this morning and made a donation to a local school this morning
Thanks
Simeon

(b)   Enter this transaction in the computer.

Task 2.5

Refer to the following email from Simeon:

---

email

From : simeon@exefactory.webnet.uk

To : accounts@exefactory.webnet.uk

Date: 6 August 2011

Subject: Opening Balances

Hi

I've just realised that the list of opening balances I gave you for entry to the new computer system contained an error. The balance of £450.00 for insurance actually contains a sum of £80.00 which should be classified as Advertising – sorry, my mistake!

Could you please correct this for me?

Thanks

Simeon

Enter the appropriate journal into the computer to correct the error in the opening balances.

Task 2.6

(a) Print a screen shot of the journal.

Task 2.7

(a) Print a trial balance.

(b) Check the accuracy of the trial balance and, if necessary, correct any errors.

Task 3.1

Refer to the following email from Simeon:

---

email

From : Simeon@exefactory.webnet.uk

To : accounts@exefactory.webnet.uk

Date: 8 August 2011

Subject: New customer

Hi

Could you please enter the details of a new customer that I have agreed terms with this morning?

The details are:

Boyles Ltd

20 Byways Lane

Grasston

GR44 6CB

The contact name is Susan Verity

The settlement terms are 14 days with a credit limit of £2,000.

Please select an appropriate Customer Account Code for this customer

Thanks

Simeon

(a)   Set up a new customer record for Boyles Ltd to open a sales ledger account with an opening balance of nil.

(b)   Print a screen shot of the new customer's record card showing the name and address details.

Task 3.2

Refer to the following sales invoices:

The ExeFactory
10 Topp Way

Disclington

DS77 9YH
"The Best Microphones, The Best Value"

INVOICE 00164
Tax Point : 6th August 2011
VAT Registration Number: 483876517

Carrie Oakey

Soprano Avenue

Hubley

HB2 9GF

Fun & Funky × 5	£30.00	£150.00
Pro Range × 5	£90.00	£450.00
		£600.00
VAT @ 20%		£120.00
TOTAL FOR PAYMENT		£720.00

Terms: 14 days

The ExeFactory
10 Topp Way

Disclington

DS77 9YH
"The Best Microphones, The Best Value"

INVOICE 00165
Tax Point : 6th August 2011
VAT Registration Number: 483876517

Boyles Ltd

20 Byways Lane

Grasston

GR44 6CB

Pro Range × 8	£90.00	£720.00
		£720.00
VAT @ 20%		£144.00
TOTAL FOR PAYMENT		£864.00

Terms: 14 days

(a) Enter the sales invoices into the computer.

Refer to the following summary of purchases invoices:

Date	Supplier Name	Invoice Number	Gross £	VAT £	Net £	Materials £	Advertising £
8/8/11	Brooks, Stein & Co	7398	1175.00	195.83	979.17		979.17
10/8/11	Lewis Ltd	LW1054	658.00	109.67	548.33	548.33	
		Total	1833.00	305.50	1527.50	548.33	979.17

(b) Enter the purchase invoices into the computer.

Refer to the following summary of payments received from customers and made to suppliers:

Cheque / BACS Receipts Listing

Date	Details	Customer	£	How Received
11/8/11	Payment of Invoice 00160 including credit note CN41	Carrie Oakey	108.00	BACS

Cheques Paid Listing

Date	Details	Supplier	£	Cheque Number
12/8/11	Payment of opening balance	Gates Ltd	1398.18	001302
12/8/11	Part-payment of opening balance	Brooks, Stein & Co	500.00	001303

(c) Enter the receipts and payments into the computer, making sure you allocate all amounts as shown in the details column.

Task 3.3

Refer to the following petty cash vouchers:

Petty Cash Voucher

Date 12 August 2011

Ref: PC 24

Details	
Train fare – exempt for VAT	£22.60
Receipt attached	

Petty Cash Voucher

Date 14 August 2011

Ref: PC 25

Details	
Printer cartridge	£19.99
VAT	£4.00
	———
Total	£23.99
	———
Receipt attached	

Enter the petty cash payments into the computer.

Task 3.4

Refer to the following e-mail from Simeon:

email
From : Simeon@Simeontimbercrafts.co.uk
To : accounts@Simeontimbercrafts.co.uk
Date: 14 August 2011
Subject: Grant

Hi

I don't know if you remember me telling you but I applied for a grant a few months ago – and guess what! We've just got a cheque through from the grant agency for £300 – I've taken it to the bank this morning when I was passing.

Could you enter it into the system please?

Thanks

Simeon

(a) Enter this grant income into the computer.

Refer to the following receipt for the purchase of a new picture, paid for out of petty cash:

Receipt Number 1331

Art of the Matter

Kitchener Shopping Centre

Miltonby

VAT Reg: 343 4839 47

Date : 14 August 2010

Received from Simeon Powell, by cash, for original print

£60 inc VAT

(b) Enter the details of this transaction into the computer. This is a picture for the office wall, so should be coded to Nominal Code 7803.

Refer to the following schedule of standing orders:

Day in month	Payee	Expense	£
15th	J Jones	Rent	500.00
16th	Disclington B. C.	Rates	160.00

Assume both of these are zero-rated.

(c) Enter the standing orders into the computer as recurring transactions being taken from the bank on the 15th of each month, and post them as necessary to ensure that August's transactions are entered into the computer.

Task 3.5

Refer to the post-it note left on your desk by Simeon shown below:

Hi

Sorry – the grant was for £350, not £300 as I said.

Simeon

Adjust the figure by making appropriate entries to the bank account.

Task 3.6

Refer to the email below from Simeon:

email
From : Simeon@exefactory.webnet.uk
To : accounts@exefactory.webnet.uk
Date: 31st August 2011
Subject: Petty cash
Hi
Please transfer the correct amount from the bank account to the petty cash account to reimburse the petty cash float – this should reinstate it to £200.00.
Thanks
Simeon

(a)   Enter this transaction into the computer.

(b)   Print the cash payments record for the petty cash account.

Task 3.7

(a)   Print a trial balance.

(b)   Check the accuracy of the trial balance and, if necessary, correct any errors.

Task 4.1

Refer to the following bank statement:

MIDWEST BANK plc
109 Church Street
Dornley
DN12 5DE

The Exe Factory
10 Topp Way
Disclington
DS77 9YH

Account Number : 17329837   31 August 2011

Statement of Account – Sheet 901

Date (2011)	Details	Paid out £	Paid in £	Balance £
1 August	Opening Balance			9218.81
05/08/2011	BGC		2031.22	11250.03
05/08/2011	BACS Receipt		8143.20	19393.23
06/08/2011	BGC		36.00	19429.23
08/08/2011	BGC		232.65	19661.88
10/08/2011	Chq 001301	2101.92		17559.96
12/08/2011	Chq 001302	2126.37		15433.59
12/08/2011	Chq 001304	1398.18		14035.41
13/08/2011	BACS Receipt		108.00	14143.41
15/08/2011	Direct Debit	500.00		13643.41
16/08/2011	Direct Debit	160.00		13483.41
18/08/2011	BGC		350.00	13833.41
28/08/2011	Bank Charges	20.00		13813.41
31/08/2011	Closing Balance			13813.41

CR = Credit
DR = Debit

(a) Enter the bank charges (no VAT) which have not yet been accounted for

(b) Reconcile the bank statement. Print out a Bank Reconciled Transactions Report. If the bank statement does not reconcile check your work and make the necessary corrections

Task 4.2

(a) Back up your work to a suitable storage media.

(b) Print a screen shot of the backup screen showing the location of back up data.

Task 4.3

Print the following reports:

- The customer invoices overdue report
- The customer activity (detailed) report
- The purchases day book (supplier invoices)

Task 4.4

(a) Generate an Aged Creditor Analysis showing all outstanding items and print a copy.

(b) Generate an Aged Debtors Analysis showing all outstanding items and print a copy.

Task 4.5

Print a Statement of Account for Carrie Oakey.

KAPLAN PUBLISHING

2 Practice Assessment Answers

Task 1.1

Customer Activity (Detailed) Report

Date: 05/02/2012   **The Exe Factory**   Page: 1
Time: 10:25:03   **Customer Activity (Detailed)**

Date From:	01/01/1980	Customer From:
Date To:	31/08/2011	Customer To: ZZZZZZZZ
Transaction From:	1	N/C From:
Transaction To:	99,999,999	N/C To: 99999999
Inc b/fwd transaction: No		Dept From: 0
Exc later payment: No		Dept To: 999

** NOTE: All report values are shown in Base Currency, unless otherwise indicated **

A/C: CO001   Name: Carrie Oakey   Contact: Carrie Oakey   Tel: 07732 389181

No	Type	Date	Ref	N/C	Details	Dept	T/C	Value	O/S	Debit	Credit	V	B
2	SI	27/07/2011	00148	9998	Opening Balance	0	T9	8,143.20 *	8,143.20	8,143.20		-	-
					Totals:			8,143.20	8,143.20	8,143.20			

Amount Outstanding   8,143.20
Amount Paid this period   0.00
Credit Limit £   10,000.00
Turnover YTD   0.00

A/C: PP002   Name: Poptastic Ltd   Contact: Lewis Welsh   Tel: 07712 381912

No	Type	Date	Ref	N/C	Details	Dept	T/C	Value	O/S	Debit	Credit	V	B
3	SI	28/07/2011	00154	9998	Opening Balance	0	T9	2,129.21 *	2,129.21	2,129.21		-	-
4	SI	30/07/2011	00157	9998	Opening Balance	0	T9	2,003.28 *	2,003.28	2,003.28		-	-
					Totals:			4,132.49	4,132.49	4,132.49			

Amount Outstanding   4,132.49
Amount Paid this period   0.00
Credit Limit £   6,000.00
Turnover YTD   0.00

A/C: SS001   Name: Sunshine Singalongs   Contact: Chelsea Curle   Tel: 01927 21873112

No	Type	Date	Ref	N/C	Details	Dept	T/C	Value	O/S	Debit	Credit	V	B
1	SI	21/07/2011	00146	9998	Opening Balance	0	T9	2,031.22 *	2,031.22	2,031.22		-	-
					Totals:			2,031.22	2,031.22	2,031.22			

Amount Outstanding   2,031.22
Amount Paid this period   0.00
Credit Limit £   4,000.00
Turnover YTD   0.00

A/C: SS002   Name: Sensational Singers Ltd   Contact: Dana Miload   Tel: 0845 217983

No	Type	Date	Ref	N/C	Details	Dept	T/C	Value	O/S	Debit	Credit	V	B
5	SI	17/04/2011	00129	9998	Opening Balance	0	T9	190.87 *	190.87	190.87		-	-
					Totals:			190.87	190.87	190.87			

Amount Outstanding   190.87
Amount Paid this period   0.00
Credit Limit £   5,000.00
Turnover YTD   0.00

Task 1.2

| Date: | 05/02/2012 | | The Exe Factory | | | Page: | 1 |

Time: 10:44:52

Supplier Activity (Detailed)

Date From:	01/01/1980		Supplier From:	
Date To:	31/08/2011		Supplier To:	ZZZZZZZZ
Transaction From:	1		N/C From:	
Transaction To:	99,999,999		N/C To:	99999999
Inc b/fwd transaction:	No		Dept From:	0
Exc later payment:	No		Dept To:	999

** NOTE: All report values are shown in Base Currency, unless otherwise indicated **

| A/C: | BS004 | Name: | Brooks, Stein & Co | | Contact: | Katherine Rose | | Tel: | 07119 010920 |

No	Type	Date	Ref	N/C	Details		Dept	T/C	Value	O/S	Debit	Credit	V	B
9	PI	20/07/2011	7326	9998	Opening Balance		0	T9	1,001.29 *	1,001.29		1,001.29	-	-
						Totals:			1,001.29	1,001.29	0.00	1,001.29		

Amount Outstanding	1,001.29
Amount paid this period	0.00
Credit Limit £	6,000.00
Turnover YTD	0.00

| A/C: | GT003 | Name: | Gates Ltd | | Contact: | Jeff Little | | Tel: | 07715 2781718 |

No	Type	Date	Ref	N/C	Details		Dept	T/C	Value	O/S	Debit	Credit	V	B
7	PI	20/07/2011	18918	9998	Opening Balance		0	T9	1,398.18 *	1,398.18		1,398.18	-	-
						Totals:			1,398.18	1,398.18	0.00	1,398.18		

Amount Outstanding	1,398.18
Amount paid this period	0.00
Credit Limit £	6,000.00
Turnover YTD	0.00

| A/C: | LL002 | Name: | Lewis Ltd | | Contact: | Emily Wills | | Tel: | 01928 238911 |

No	Type	Date	Ref	N/C	Details		Dept	T/C	Value	O/S	Debit	Credit	V	B

*** No Transactions ***

| A/C: | WD002 | Name: | Wardshayne Ltd | | Contact: | Majid Singh | | Tel: | 02618 1818910 |

No	Type	Date	Ref	N/C	Details		Dept	T/C	Value	O/S	Debit	Credit	V	B
6	PI	18/07/2011	189	9998	Opening Balance		0	T9	2,126.37 *	2,126.37		2,126.37	-	-
						Totals:			2,126.37	2,126.37	0.00	2,126.37		

Amount Outstanding	2,126.37
Amount paid this period	0.00
Credit Limit £	5,000.00
Turnover YTD	0.00

| A/C: | YG001 | Name: | Young & Co | | Contact: | Robin Maclay | | Tel: | 0845 1398232 |

No	Type	Date	Ref	N/C	Details		Dept	T/C	Value	O/S	Debit	Credit	V	B
8	PI	12/07/2011	YG1089	9998	Opening Balance		0	T9	2,101.92 *	2,101.92		2,101.92	-	-
						Totals:			2,101.92	2,101.92	0.00	2,101.92		

Amount Outstanding	2,101.92
Amount paid this period	0.00
Credit Limit £	4,000.00
Turnover YTD	0.00

Task 1.3

This is a data input task so no answer given.

Task 1.4

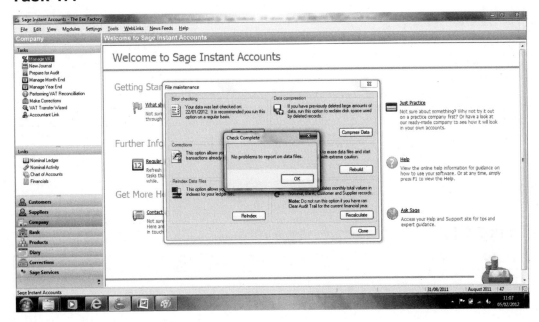

Task 1.5

Date:	05/02/2012	**The Exe Factory**		**Page:** 1
Time:	11:17:23	**Period Trial Balance**		

To Period: Month 12, July 2012

N/C	Name	Debit	Credit
0020	Plant and Machinery	92,420.12	
0030	Office Equipment	4,219.35	
0050	Motor Vehicles	12,400.98	
1100	Debtors Control Account	14,497.78	
1200	Bank Current Account	9,218.81	
1230	Petty Cash	200.00	
2100	Creditors Control Account		6,627.76
2200	Sales Tax Control Account		15,212.61
2201	Purchase Tax Control Account	7,524.31	
3000	Capital		25,000.00
3200	Profit and Loss Account		55,681.39
4000	Sales - Fun and Funky		38,120.19
4001	Sales - Pro Range		29,108.62
4002	Cash Sales		16,210.40
5000	Materials Purchased	38,734.19	
6201	Advertising	1,480.32	
7100	Rent and Rates	1,100.00	
7104	Insurance	450.00	
7203	Heat and Light	1,729.82	
7304	Miscellaneous Motor Expenses	1,092.93	
7504	Office Stationery	892.36	
	Totals:	185,960.97	185,960.97

Task 2.1 (a)

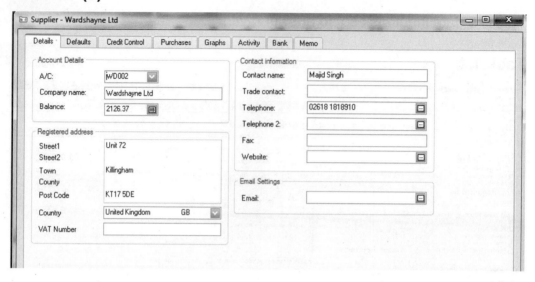

Task 2.1 (c)

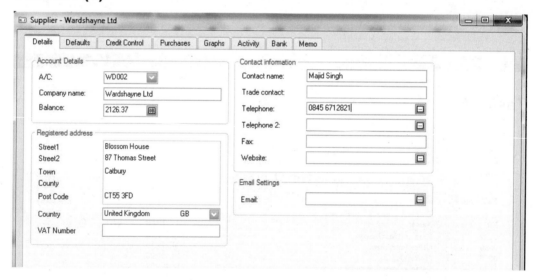

Task 2.2 (d)

The Exe Factory
10 Topp Way
Disclington
DS77 9YH

PP002

Poptastic Ltd   05/02/2012
Caruso Industrial Estate

Mellingham

ML21 9GF

All values are shown in   Pound Sterling

28/07/2011	00154	Goods/Services	£	2,129.21	£	2,129.21
30/07/2011	00157	Goods/Services	£	2,003.28	£	4,132.49
01/08/2011	00162	Goods/Services	£	831.60	£	4,964.09

£	0.00	£	0.00	£	0.00	£	0.00	£ 4,964.09	**£ 4,964.09**

The Exe Factory
10 Topp Way
Disclington
DS77 9YH

PP002

Poptastic Ltd   05/02/2012
Caruso Industrial Estate

Mellingham

ML21 9GF

All values are shown in   Pound Sterling

28/07/2011	00154	Goods/Services	£	2,129.21		£	2,129.21
30/07/2011	00157	Goods/Services	£	2,003.28		£	4,132.49
01/08/2011	00162	Goods/Services	£	831.60		£	4,964.09
05/08/2011	BADDBT	Credit			£ 4,964.09	£	0.00

£ 0.00	£ 0.00	£ 0.00	£ 0.00	£ 0.00		£ **0.00**

Task 2.6

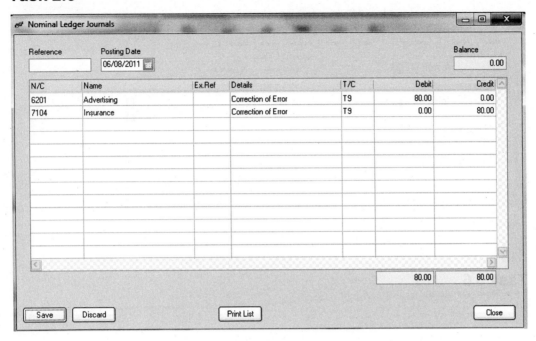

Task 2.7

Date: 05/02/2012
Time: 14:58:57

The Exe Factory

Period Trial Balance

Page: 1

To Period: Month 12, July 2012

N/C	Name	Debit	Credit
0020	Plant and Machinery	92,420.12	
0030	Office Equipment	4,219.35	
0050	Motor Vehicles	12,400.98	
1100	Debtors Control Account	1,774.87	
1200	Bank Current Account	15,408.59	
1230	Petty Cash	147.55	
2100	Creditors Control Account		3,224.36
2200	Sales Tax Control Account		15,659.98
2201	Purchase Tax Control Account	7,668.03	
3000	Capital		25,000.00
3200	Profit and Loss Account		55,681.39
4000	Sales - Fun and Funky		38,450.19
4001	Sales - Pro Range		30,791.62
4002	Cash Sales		16,434.28
5000	Materials Purchased	39,165.02	
6201	Advertising	1,560.32	
7100	Rent and Rates	1,100.00	
7104	Insurance	370.00	
7203	Heat and Light	1,729.82	
7304	Miscellaneous Motor Expenses	1,092.93	
7504	Office Stationery	892.36	
7601	Audit and Accountancy Fees	256.58	
7801	Cleaning	15.00	
7803	Premises Expenses	31.21	
8100	Bad Debt Write Off	4,964.09	
8200	Donations	25.00	
	Totals:	185,241.82	185,241.82

Task 3.1

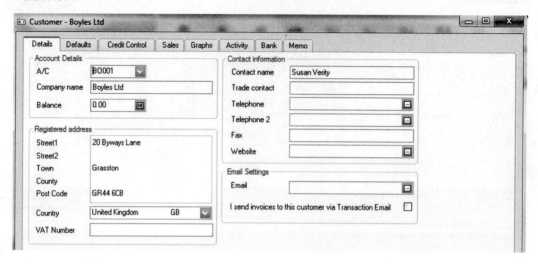

Task 3.6

Date:	05/02/2012			The Exe Factory						Page:	1	
Time:	15:33:49			Day Books: Cash Payments (Detailed)								

Date From:	01/01/1980	Bank From:	1230
DateTo:	31/12/2019	Bank To:	1230

Transaction From:	1	N/C From:	
Transaction To:	99,999,999	N/C To:	99999999

Dept From:	0
Dept To:	999

Bank: 1230 Currency: Pound Sterling

No	Type	N/C	Date	Ref	Details	Dept	Net £	Tax £	T/C	Gross £	V	B	Bank Rec. Date
62	CP	7801	03/08/2011	PC22	Window Cleaning	0	15.00	0.00	T0	15.00	N	-	
63	CP	7803	06/08/2011	PC23	Pot Plants	0	31.21	6.24	T1	37.45	N	-	
77	CP	7400	12/08/2011	PC24'	Train fare	0	22.60	0.00	T2	22.60	N	-	
78	CP	7504	14/08/2011	PC25	Printer Cartridge	0	19.99	4.00	T1	23.99	N	-	
80	CP	7803	14/08/2011	1331	Picture	0	50.00	10.00	T1	60.00	N	-	
						Totals £	138.80	20.24		159.04			

Task 3.7

Date: 05/02/2012
Time: 15:35:51

The Exe Factory
Period Trial Balance

Page: 1

To Period: Month 12, July 2012

N/C	Name	Debit	Credit
0020	Plant and Machinery	92,420.12	
0030	Office Equipment	4,219.35	
0050	Motor Vehicles	12,400.98	
1100	Debtors Control Account	3,250.87	
1200	Bank Current Account	13,149.37	
1230	Petty Cash	200.00	
2100	Creditors Control Account		3,159.18
2200	Sales Tax Control Account		15,923.98
2201	Purchase Tax Control Account	7,987.53	
3000	Capital		25,000.00
3200	Profit and Loss Account		55,681.39
4000	Sales - Fun and Funky		38,600.19
4001	Sales - Pro Range		31,961.62
4002	Cash Sales		16,434.28
4900	Miscellaneous Income		350.00
5000	Materials Purchased	39,713.35	
6201	Advertising	2,539.49	
7100	Rent and Rates	1,760.00	
7104	Insurance	370.00	
7203	Heat and Light	1,729.82	
7304	Miscellaneous Motor Expenses	1,092.93	
7400	Travelling	22.60	
7504	Office Stationery	912.35	
7601	Audit and Accountancy Fees	256.58	
7801	Cleaning	15.00	
7803	Premises Expenses	81.21	
8100	Bad Debt Write Off	4,964.09	
8200	Donations	25.00	
	Totals:	187,110.64	187,110.64

Task 4.1 (b)

Date: 05/02/2012
Time: 15:57:04

The Exe Factory
Bank Reconciled Transactions

Page: 1

Bank Reconciled On:31/08/2011

No	Type	Date	A/C	N/C	Dept	Ref	Details	Net	Tax	T/C
16	JD	01/08/2011	1200	1200	0	O/Bal	Opening Balance	9,218.81	0.00	T9
57	SR	04/08/2011	CO001	1200	0	BACS	Sales Receipt	8,143.20	0.00	T9
58	SR	05/08/2011	SS001	1200	0	CHEQUE	Sales Receipt	2,031.22	0.00	T9
59	PP	04/08/2011	YG001	1200	0	001301	Purchase Payment	2,101.92	0.00	T9
60	PP	04/08/2011	WD002	1200	0	001302	Purchase Payment	2,126.37	0.00	T9
64	BR	02/08/2011	1200	4002	0	369		30.00	6.00	T1
65	BR	06/08/2011	1200	4002	0	370		193.88	38.77	T1
74	SR	11/08/2011	CO001	1200	0	BACS	Sales Receipt	108.00	0.00	T9
75	PP	12/08/2011	GT003	1200	0	001302	Purchase Payment	1,398.18	0.00	T9
79	BR	14/08/2011	1200	4900	0		Grant	350.00	0.00	T9
81	BP	15/08/2011	1200	7100	0	DD/STO		500.00	0.00	T0
82	BP	15/08/2011	1200	7100	0	DD/STO		160.00	0.00	T0
86	BP	28/08/2011	1200	7901	0		Bank Charges	20.00	0.00	T9

Task 4.2 (b)

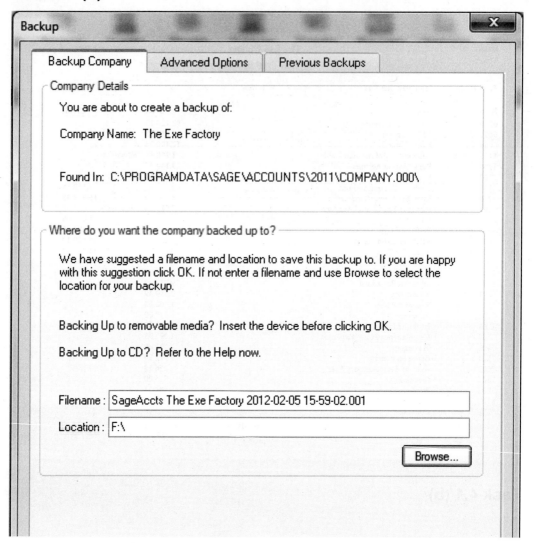

Task 4.3

Date:	05/02/2012							Page:	1
Time:	16:00:26		**The Exe Factory**						
			Customer Invoices Overdue						

Customer From:						DateFrom:	01/01/1980
Customer To:	ZZZZZZZZ					DateTo:	05/02/2012
Transaction From:	1					Exc Later Payments:	No
Transaction To:	99,999,999						

A/C:	BO001	Name:	Boyles Ltd		Contact:	Susan Verity		Tel:	
No	**Type**	**Date**	**Due Date**	**Ref**	**Details**	**Amount**	**Paid**	**Outstanding**	
71	SI	06/08/2011	20/08/2011	00165	8 x Pro	864.00	0.00	864.00	
							Total:	864.00	

A/C:	CO001	Name:	Carrie Oakay		Contact:	Carrie Oakay		Tel:	07732 389181
No	**Type**	**Date**	**Due Date**	**Ref**	**Details**	**Amount**	**Paid**	**Outstanding**	
69	SI	06/08/2011	03/09/2011	00164	5 x F&F	720.00	0.00	720.00	
							Total:	720.00	

A/C:	SS001	Name:	Sunshine Singalongs		Contact:	Chelsea Curle		Tel:	01927 21873112
No	**Type**	**Date**	**Due Date**	**Ref**	**Details**	**Amount**	**Paid**	**Outstanding**	
51	SI	05/08/2011	02/09/2011	00163	8 x F&F	1,476.00	0.00	1,476.00	
							Total:	1,476.00	

A/C:	SS002	Name:	Sensational Singers Ltd		Contact:	Dana Miload		Tel:	0845 217983
No	**Type**	**Date**	**Due Date**	**Ref**	**Details**	**Amount**	**Paid**	**Outstanding**	
5	SI	17/04/2011	15/05/2011	00129	Opening Balance	190.87	0.00	190.87	
							Total:	190.87	
							Grand Total:	3,250.87	

Date:	05/02/2012			**The Exe Factory**				Page:	1
Time:	16:04:11			**Customer Activity (Detailed)**					

Date From:	01/01/1980				Customer From:	
Date To:	05/02/2012				Customer To:	ZZZZZZZZ
Transaction From:	1				N/C From:	
Transaction To:	99,999,999				N/C To:	99999999
Inc b/fwd transaction:	No				Dept From:	0
Exc later payment:	No				Dept To:	999

** NOTE: All report values are shown in Base Currency, unless otherwise indicated **

A/C:	BO001	Name:	Boyles Ltd			Contact:	Susan Verity		Tel:			
No	**Type**	**Date**	**Ref**	**N/C**	**Details**	**Dept**	**T/C**	**Value**	**O/S**	**Debit**	**Credit**	**V B**
71	SI	06/08/2011	00165	4001	8 x Pro	0	T1	864.00 *	864.00	864.00		N -
						Totals:		864.00	864.00	864.00		

Amount Outstanding	864.00
Amount Paid this period	0.00
Credit Limit £	2,000.00
Turnover YTD	720.00

A/C:	CO001	Name:	Carrie Oakay			Contact:	Carrie Oakay		Tel:	07732 389181		
No	**Type**	**Date**	**Ref**	**N/C**	**Details**	**Dept**	**T/C**	**Value**	**O/S**	**Debit**	**Credit**	**V B**
2	SI	27/07/2011	00148	9998	Opening Balance	0	T9	8,143.20		8,143.20		- -
48	SI	01/08/2011	00160	4000	3 x F&F	0	T1	108.00		108.00		N -
49	SI	01/08/2011	00160	4001	1 x Pro	0	T1	118.80		118.80		N -
53	SC	02/08/2011	41	4001	1 x Pro	0	T1	118.80			118.80	N -
57	SR	04/08/2011	BACS	1200	Sales Receipt	0	T9	8,143.20			8,143.20	- -
69	SI	06/08/2011	00164	4000	5 x F&F	0	T1	180.00 *	180.00	180.00		N -
70	SI	06/08/2011	00164	4001	5 x Pro	0	T1	540.00 *	540.00	540.00		N -
74	SR	11/08/2011	BACS	1200	Sales Receipt	0	T9	108.00			108.00	- R
						Totals:		720.00	720.00	9,090.00	8,370.00	

Amount Outstanding	720.00
Amount Paid this period	8,251.20
Credit Limit £	10,000.00
Turnover YTD	690.00

A/C:	PP002	Name:	Poptastic Ltd			Contact:	Lewis Walsh		Tel:	07712 381912		
No	**Type**	**Date**	**Ref**	**N/C**	**Details**	**Dept**	**T/C**	**Value**	**O/S**	**Debit**	**Credit**	**V B**
3	SI	28/07/2011	00154	9998	Opening Balance	0	T9	2,129.21		2,129.21		- -
4	SI	30/07/2011	00157	9998	Opening Balance	0	T9	2,003.28		2,003.28		- -
50	SI	01/08/2011	00162	4001	7 x Pro	0	T1	831.60		831.60		N -
61	SC	05/08/2011	BADDBT	8100	Bad Debt Write Off	0	T9	4,964.09			4,964.09	- -
						Totals:		0.00	0.00	4,964.09	4,964.09	

Amount Outstanding	0.00
Amount Paid this period	0.00
Credit Limit £	6,000.00
Turnover YTD	693.00

A/C:	SS001	Name:	Sunshine Singalongs			Contact:	Chelsea Curle		Tel:	01927 21873112		
No	**Type**	**Date**	**Ref**	**N/C**	**Details**	**Dept**	**T/C**	**Value**	**O/S**	**Debit**	**Credit**	**V B**
1	SI	21/07/2011	00146	9998	Opening Balance	0	T9	2,031.22		2,031.22		- -
51	SI	05/08/2011	00163	4000	8 x F&F	0	T1	288.00 *	288.00	288.00		N -
52	SI	05/08/2011	00163	4001	10 x Pro	0	T1	1,188.00 *	1,188.00	1,188.00		N -
58	SR	05/08/2011	CHEQUE	1200	Sales Receipt	0	T9	2,031.22			2,031.22	- R
						Totals:		1,476.00	1,476.00	3,507.22	2,031.22	

Amount Outstanding	1,476.00
Amount Paid this period	2,031.22
Credit Limit £	4,000.00
Turnover YTD	1,230.00

Date:	05/02/2012			**The Exe Factory**				Page:	2
Time:	16:04:11			**Customer Activity (Detailed)**					

A/C:	SS002	Name:	Sensational Singers Ltd			Contact:	Dana Miload		Tel:	0845 217983		
No	**Type**	**Date**	**Ref**	**N/C**	**Details**	**Dept**	**T/C**	**Value**	**O/S**	**Debit**	**Credit**	**V B**
5	SI	17/04/2011	00129	9998	Opening Balance	0	T9	190.87 *	190.87	190.87		- -
						Totals:		190.87	190.87	190.87		

Amount Outstanding	190.87
Amount Paid this period	0.00
Credit Limit £	5,000.00
Turnover YTD	0.00

Date: 05/02/2012   **The Exe Factory**   Page: 1
Time: 16:05:33

Day Books: Supplier Invoices (Detailed)

Date From:	01/01/1980						Supplier From:	
Date To:	31/12/2019						Supplier To:	ZZZZZZZZ
Transaction From:	1						N/C From:	
Transaction To:	99,999,999						N/C To:	99999999
Dept From:	0							
Dept To:	999							

Tran No.	Type	Date	A/C Ref	N/C	Inv Ref	Dept	Details	Net Amount	Tax Amount	T/C	Gross Amount	V	B
6	PI	18/07/2011	WD002	9998	189	0	Opening Balance	2,126.37	0.00	T9	2,126.37	-	-
7	PI	20/07/2011	GT003	9998	18918	0	Opening Balance	1,398.18	0.00	T9	1,398.18	-	-
8	PI	12/07/2011	YG001	9998	YG1089	0	Opening Balance	2,101.92	0.00	T9	2,101.92	-	-
9	PI	20/07/2011	BS004	9998	7326	0	Opening Balance	1,001.29	0.00	T9	1,001.29	-	-
54	PI	03/08/2011	YG001	7601	YG1120	0	Accounting	256.58	51.31	T1	307.89	N	-
55	PI	04/08/2011	LL002	5000	1918	0	Materials	352.50	70.50	T1	423.00	N	-
56	PI	05/08/2011	WD002	5000	218	0	Materials	78.33	15.67	T1	94.00	N	-
72	PI	08/08/2011	BS004	6201	7398	0	Advertising	979.17	195.83	T1	1,175.00	N	-
73	PI	10/08/2011	LL002	5000	LW1054	0	Materials	548.33	109.67	T1	658.00	N	-
							Totals	**8,842.67**	**442.98**		**9,285.65**		

Task 4.4

Date: 05/02/2012   **The Exe Factory**   Page: 1
Time: 16:13:43

Aged Creditors Analysis (Summary)

Report Date:	05/02/2012							Supplier From:	
Include future transactions:	No							Supplier To:	ZZZZZZZZ
Exclude Later Payments:	No								

** NOTE: All report values are shown in Base Currency, unless otherwise indicated **

A/C	Name	Credit Limit	Turnover	Balance	Future	Current	Period 1	Period 2	Period 3	Older
BS004	Brooks, Stein & Co	£ 6,000.00	979.17	1,676.29	0.00	0.00	0.00	0.00	0.00	1,676.29
LL002	Lewis Ltd	£ 1,000.00	900.83	1,081.00	0.00	0.00	0.00	0.00	0.00	1,081.00
WD002	Wardshayne Ltd	£ 5,000.00	78.33	94.00	0.00	0.00	0.00	0.00	0.00	94.00
YG001	Young & Co	£ 4,000.00	256.58	307.89	0.00	0.00	0.00	0.00	0.00	307.89
	Totals:		**2,214.91**	**3,159.18**	**0.00**	**0.00**	**0.00**	**0.00**	**0.00**	**3,159.18**

Date: 05/02/2012   **The Exe Factory**   Page: 1
Time: 16:15:40

Aged Debtors Analysis (Summary)

Report Date:	05/02/2012							Customer From:	
Include future transactions:	No							Customer To:	ZZZZZZZZ
Exclude later payments:	No								

** NOTE: All report values are shown in Base Currency, unless otherwise indicated **

A/C	Name	Credit Limit	Turnover	Balance	Future	Current	Period 1	Period 2	Period 3	Older
BO001	Boyles Ltd	£ 2,000.00	720.00	864.00	0.00	0.00	0.00	0.00	0.00	864.00
CO001	Carrie Oakey	£ 10,000.00	690.00	720.00	0.00	0.00	0.00	0.00	0.00	720.00
SS001	Sunshine Singalongs	£ 4,000.00	1,230.00	1,476.00	0.00	0.00	0.00	0.00	0.00	1,476.00
SS002	Sensational Singers Ltd	£ 5,000.00	0.00	190.87	0.00	0.00	0.00	0.00	0.00	190.87
	Totals:		**2,640.00**	**3,250.87**	**0.00**	**0.00**	**0.00**	**0.00**	**0.00**	**3,250.87**

Task 4.5

The Exe Factory
10 Topp Way
Disclington
DS77 9YH

CO001

Carrie Oakey   05/02/2012
Soprano Avenue

Hubley

HB2 9GF

All values are shown in Pound Sterling

27/07/2011	00148	Goods/Services	£	8,143.20			£	8,143.20
01/08/2011	00160	Goods/Services	£	226.80			£	8,370.00
02/08/2011	41	Credit			£	118.80	£	8,251.20
04/08/2011	BACS	Payment			£	8,143.20	£	108.00
06/08/2011	00164	Goods/Services	£	720.00			£	828.00
11/08/2011	BACS	Payment			£	108.00	£	720.00

£	0.00	£	0.00	£	0.00	£	0.00	£	720.00		£	**720.00**

INDEX